THE VOLUNTEER BOOK

A GUIDE FOR CHURCHES AND NONPROFITS

DENISE LOCKER

BEACON HILL PRESS
OF KANSAS CITY

Library of Congress Cataloging-in-Publication Data

Locker, Denise, 1953-
    The volunteer book : a guide for churches and nonprofits / Denise Locker.
        p. cm.
    Includes bibliographical references (p.   ).
    ISBN 978-0-8341-2494-3 (pbk.)
    1. Voluntarism—Religious aspects—Christianity. 2. Church management. 3. Voluntarism. 4. Nonprofit organizations—Management. I. Title.
    BR115.V64L63 2010
    254—dc22

                                                                    2009050849

CONTENTS

WHY USE VOLUNTEERS?

Snowflakes melt alone—but together they can be traffic-stoppers!
—Anonymous

Richard Bonvini is pretty proud of his grandson's passion for sports. The retired Framingham firefighter and his grandson play table tennis, bocce, and bowl together. He's attended almost all of thirteen-year-old Derek Cicciu's hockey and baseball games. But something was bothering Bonvini. He said, "My grandson, like many kids his age, had the wrong impression of what a hero is. He thought a hero was anyone who could hit a ball."

When Bonvini saw a notice in the newspaper asking for volunteers to replace flags on veterans' graves, he knew what to do. He invited his grandson to join him in replacing the nation's symbol on over 1,200 graves, including the grave of Cicciu's great-great grandfather. "I taught my grandson that these are your heroes," Bonvini said.[1]

I Touch Each Person

Helen Mauck helps her church by stuffing inserts into the Sunday bulletins. Helen says, "My motivation to volunteer comes from a desire to serve the Lord. I have a full-time job, so my challenge is finding a time to serve that fits with my work schedule. Stuffing bulletins slips easily into the time I have available.

"I enjoy serving with the women who are older than me, visiting with them, and learning from their experiences as we work. By touching each bulletin and insert, I feel as if I'm serving each person in the church who receives a bulletin on Sunday, members and visitors alike.

"Another motivation for me is that I'm able to help the church secretary by freeing her time to do other things."

These are just two examples that illustrate the value of volunteers and provide a glimpse into the kind of individuals who might get involved with your organization.

Before we move into the details of how to start, grow, and maintain a volunteer program, let's first look at the biblical view of volunteers, or as the Bible calls them, "servants."

Biblical Backdrop for Today's Volunteers

When Jesus completed His assignment on earth and returned to heaven, He left His work in the hands of volunteers. After Jesus' death and resurrection, the eleven chosen disciples went to the spot where Jesus had told them He would meet them. Even though they had seen Him since His resurrection, they were still overcome and worshiped Him on the spot.

Jesus' words to them—and to us—were given as a charge as they began their volunteer ministry. According to Matthew 28:18-20, Jesus said, "All authority has been given to Me in heaven and on earth. Go therefore and make disciples of all the nations, baptizing them in the name of the Father and of the Son and of the Holy Spirit, teaching them to observe all things that I have commanded you; and lo, I am with you always, even to the end of the age" (NKJV).

The word *servant* occurs in various forms over 1,100 times in the Bible. The Greek word *doulos* is used to describe Moses in Revelation 15:3, Paul in Titus 1:1, and James in James 1:1. Both Paul and James refer to themselves as servants of God; Paul also calls himself the "servant of Christ" in Romans 1:1 and Philippians 1:1. The definition of the term *doulos* is slave or bondman. Another way to express it is as one who gives himself or herself up to another's will, whose service is used by Christ in extending and advancing His cause among humanity.

An additional Greek term used eight times in the New Testament is *douloo*. The definition is similar but slightly different. It means to make a slave of, reduce to bondage, give oneself wholly to another's needs and service, and make oneself a bondsman to him. This word is used in 1 Corinthians 9:19, where Paul states, "Though I am free from all men, I have made myself a servant to all, that I might win the more" (NKJV). Being a servant of God is a choice.

At Habitat for Humanity volunteers are classified as staff. We make the distinction between paid and unpaid staff. We do our best to match skills with tasks. We hold everyone to similar standards. It is our obligation to provide training and guidance to everyone who works for us. When staff is working out of compassion for people, or passion for the mission, it distinguishes them from those who are working to feed their families. I am fortunate to have a very passionate and dedicated group of people.

—Anita Hellam, Habitat for Humanity

Paul worked as a tentmaker in order to be self-supporting. This labor enabled him to volunteer, freeing him to serve. Acts 18:2-4 conveys how Paul became friends with Aquila and his wife, Priscilla. Verse 3 tells us that Paul "was of the same trade, he stayed with them and worked; for by occupation they were tentmakers." But tent-making wasn't his primary focus. Verse 4 continues, "and he reasoned in the synagogue every Sabbath, and persuaded both Jews and Greeks."

Paul invested a great deal of time and energy in developing young Timothy for service. In 2 Timothy 4:1-2 Paul spells out to Timothy that our call to service is from God. Inspired by the

Holy Spirit, Paul gives Timothy his job description: "Preach the word! Be ready in season and out of season. Convince, rebuke, exhort, with all longsuffering and teaching." All these men of faith were volunteers.

Old Testament Example

One excellent example in the Old Testament that demonstrates the use of volunteers is Moses. Through his father-in-law, God directed Moses to form a leadership structure to carry out the task of mediation between the people. In Exodus 18:17-23, Moses' father-in law, Jethro, watches Moses spend numerous hours meeting with the people, trying to help them resolve their conflicts and mediate their issues. After observing this, Jethro approaches Moses and tells him that this is not a good thing for Moses or the people. The task is too much for any single person; Moses needs to share his load. Jethro then proceeds to tell Moses exactly what he should do and breaks it down into practical steps in Exodus 18:21-23:

> Moreover you shall select from all the people able men, such as fear God, men of truth, hating covetousness; and place such over them to be rulers of thousands, rulers of hundreds, rulers of fifties, and rulers of tens. And let them judge the people at all times. Then it will be that every great matter they shall bring to you, but every small matter they themselves shall judge. So it will be easier for you, for they will bear the burden with you. If you do this thing, and God so commands you, then you will be able to endure, and all this people will also go to their place in peace (NKJV).

Moses was able to see the wisdom of Jethro's statements and did as his father-in-law instructed, dividing the people into groups of thousands, hundreds, fifties, and tens. When he appointed leaders over each of these groups, the plan was very successful for Moses and the people. These leaders were all volunteers through whom God provided the solution for Moses' problem and the structure for continued success.

Support Behind the Lines

Another Old Testament illustration of servanthood is found in Exodus 17:8-13, in which two men stepped up to "support" Moses. The Israelites had been drawn into a battle by the Amalekites. Moses told Joshua, "Choose us some men and go out, fight with Amalek" (verse 9). Nothing too strange there, but then Moses tells Joshua that he will stand on the top of the hill with the rod of God. Joshua agrees and goes out with his troops to fight with the Amalekites.

Here comes the interesting part. As long as Moses held up the rod of God, Joshua and Israel prevailed in the battle. But just how long can you reasonably hold your arms up? When Moses' arms grew tired, and he inevitably lowered the rod of God, the Amalekite army prevailed. Moses became so weary attempting to hold up the rod of God that another solution had to be found.

Volunteers are the lifeblood of nonprofits. The boards of trustees are volunteers, docents are volunteers.
 —Leo H. Cullum, current volunteer St. Vincent De Paul Village, former Director of Mission Advancement Medical Ambassadors International

What happened next is a wonderful illustration of servanthood. Verses 12-13 reveal that "Aaron and Hur supported his hands, one on one side, and the other on the other side; and his hands were steady until the going down of the sun. So Joshua defeated Amalek and his people with the edge of the sword."

Like Moses, we should not be ashamed about needing or asking for help from others. Nor should we be timid about providing the help others may need. The old adage is true that many hands make light work. Needing help is not an indictment against our abilities. It is simply an acknowledgement that we can accomplish more working together. Moses was God's man, but he needed the service of others to support him. Aaron and Hur's assistance strengthened Moses to perform the task God had placed before him.

The principle is the same with volunteers today. They come alongside an organization or church to help fulfill the tasks God has called them to carry out. By failing to utilize their help and strengths, we're overlooking a valuable resource and robbing them of the opportunity to serve.

Jesus, Our Model

The prime example of servanthood is, of course, that of Jesus himself. A key verse is Mark 10:45 NIV:

> For even the Son of Man did not come to be served, but to serve, and to give His life as a ransom for many.

Jesus stands as a beacon guiding us away from a self-seeking lifestyle and demonstrating by His life and example how He desires us to live—how He desires us to serve.

These biblical examples, along with many others, emphasize the importance of a servant heart, attitude, and lifestyle. It is imperative to live these examples ourselves and cultivate them within our churches and organizations. Each of us has the ability to impact others and along the way accomplish many God-given assignments.

Recap

- *Volunteerism/servanthood is important in the Bible.* Many examples throughout Scripture illustrate the concept of servanthood and how we should be living, thus encouraging service in others.
- *There is a need.* On any given weekend more than forty-seven percent of the United States' population attends church. Baby Boomers attend church at the rate of forty-nine per-

cent, with the older generation attending at fifty-four percent.[2] It is estimated that there are more than 330,000 churches in the United States[3] and 1,478,197 nonprofit organizations.[4]

- *Budgets are tight.* Every organization has the need to continue operating and to complete its work within a budget—a budget that has gotten a lot tighter in the last few years. Across the board, donations have fallen, thus impacting organizations to the point that many are downsizing or closing their doors.

- *Groups of people have time on their hands.* An estimated seventy-nine million Baby Boomers turned sixty in 2006 and will reach retirement age by 2011. Many of these individuals wish to remain useful or feel appreciated and would enjoy the opportunity to work with or represent an organization with a shared belief or purpose. In addition, there are individuals whose talents are sitting idle who, if asked, would love to serve and help tell the great stories of these organizations.

The best way to find yourself is to lose yourself in the service of others.
—Gandhi

HOW DO VOLUNTEERS CONTRIBUTE?

Service is never a simple act; it's about sacrifice on behalf of others and about accomplishment for ourselves, about reaching out, one person to another, about all our choices gathered together as a country to reach across all our divides.
—George H. W. Bush

I believe there are two main methods in which a volunteer contributes to an organization. The first is by accomplishing needed tasks. The second is by functioning as an ambassador—not to be confused with being a potential fundraiser, although it may have the same results. Let's look at the task side of volunteering first.

Accomplishing Tasks

Volunteers are not intended to serve as slaves to an organization. As silly as it may seem to remind people of that, I've seen volunteers abused to the point they quit serving with an organization, or if the organization is a large one, they decided to serve in a different department. The volunteer's service should be meaningful to the organization as well as to the volunteer. There should be a sense that the work the volunteer is accomplishing is important and needed.

Below is a list of activities put together by the United States Department of Labor Bureau of Labor Statistics, last modified in February 2008. To view the full report go to <www.bls.gov/ news.release/volun.htm> and match your organization's needs with the volunteers who possess the gifts and abilities that best suit your organization. This information can benefit you as you recruit volunteers.

- *Coaches, referees, or supervisors of sports teams.* Men are more likely than women to participate in this area. These men usually have children younger than eighteen.
- *Tutors or teachers.* Women tutor more than men. Most of these women are between twenty and forty-four years of age with the largest number in the thirty-five to forty-four age bracket.
- *Mentors of youth.* Youth mentors are largely made up of singles between the ages of sixteen and nineteen. This group is closely divided between women and men.
- *Ushers, greeters, or ministers.* Men are a little more likely than women to hold the position of usher, greeter, or minister. The primary age group is fifty-five to sixty-four. This group is equally divided between singles and married.
- *Volunteers who collect, prepare, distribute, or serve food.* Women usually outnumber men in this group, which tends to be comprised of older adults.
- *Volunteers who collect, make, and distribute clothing, crafts, or other nonfood goods.* Women outpace the men in this task. The largest age group is over sixty-five years.
- *Volunteers involved in fundraising or selling items to raise money.* More women than men perform this task. The age groups break into two distinct categories: ages sixteen to nineteen and thirty-five to fifty-four.
- *Volunteers who provide counseling, medical care, fire, emergency medical services, and protective services.* Men slightly outnumber women

in this category. The primary age group is twenty to twenty-four years.

- *Volunteers who provide general office services.* Women tend to participate in this activity more than men. The average age of the volunteer here is over sixty-five years.
- *Volunteers who provide professional or management assistance, including serving on a board or committee.* Men outpace women in this group and are between fifty-five and sixty-four years old and have earned a bachelor's degree or higher. They typically do not have children under eighteen years of age.
- *Volunteers engaged in music, performance, or other artistic activities.* More men than women participate in this category. The main age group is sixteen to twenty-four years.
- *Volunteers engaged in supplying transportation to people.* Men are better represented than women here. The main age group is sixteen to twenty-four years.

What Will the Volunteers Do?

It is crucial to take the time at the outset of developing your volunteer program to involve your staff in the process of creating a list of potential volunteer functions. Your list of tasks will correlate directly with your staff's input.

From the staff's involvement you will create a "Volunteer Questionnaire." A sample of the complete form can be found in chapter 10, but the bottom section of the form is shown here. It was created directly from staff input, with the exception of the first two items under "Miscellaneous." Those items have been included to help determine the style of involvement each volunteer prefers. For instance, you wouldn't want a person who enjoys working in a group to feel exiled and alone if assigned to work independently.

Also, a blank line is found under "Office" and "Software Experience" to allow the new volunteer to include accomplishments or skills that are not included in the lists. Each new vol-

---

Area of interest: (Check as many as apply. If you have any questions about what is involved with any of the areas, please feel free to ask)

Miscellaneous	Office	Software Experience
( ) Group work	( ) Computer work	( ) Word
( ) Working individually	( ) Filing	( ) Excel
( ) Research work	( ) Proofreading	( ) Photoshop (version __)
( ) Driving to & from airport	( ) Copy work	( ) MS Outlook
___ Modesto	( ) Telephoning	( ) PageMaker (version __)
___ San Francisco	( ) Fill in on phones	( ) PowerPoint
___ Sacramento	( ) Clerical support	( ) _____
( ) Housing visitors	( ) Bulk mailing work	
( ) Accounting interest	( ) Photo scanning	
( ) Fundraising interest	( ) _____	
( ) Fix-it person		
( ) Set up/take down for events		

---

unteer should fill out a questionnaire on his or her first day with your organization.

As a sidenote: don't forget during your discussion time with new volunteers to ask them if they have any talents or experience in areas not included on the list. You might be amazed by the other talents and gifts that come your way.

Once a year it's a good idea to send an e-mail or take a few minutes during a staff meeting to find out if there are any new volunteer needs within the office. Your staff questionnaire should be updated yearly, since some tasks will no longer be necessary, and there may be new tasks for which volunteers are needed. Each list should be tailored to your organization's needs through a process of discovery involving your staff.

Unexpected Benefit for Service—Tax Break

At a nonprofit organization where I once worked, every time a volunteer came to serve, he or she signed in and out, using a binder located on the receptionist's desk. The forms we used had four columns for (1) the volunteer's name, (2) the volunteer's check-in time, (3) the volunteer's check-out time, and (4) the number of hours the volunteer served that day. Lowell Andrews, a volunteer on the leadership team, collected this information and maintained a spreadsheet to track individual volunteer hours and corporate hours. Lowell tallied cumulative volunteer hours as high as 5,000 per year. These hours equate to income for the organization as gifts-in-kind. This income is included on the organization's annual Form 990 tax report. The total number of hours volunteers served each year was reported at the annual volunteer appreciation event.

An additional benefit of maintaining a sign-up sheet was an awareness of who was in the building at all times. During a fire drill or a real emergency evacuation, the sign-in binder could be grabbed on the way out of the building and used to account for the safety of each volunteer.

Organization Types

The types of organizations where volunteer activities are performed are as follows—civic or political: 5.1 percent; educational: 26.2 percent; environmental or animal care: 1.9 percent; hospital and health: 7.8 percent; public safety: 1.3 percent; religious: 35.6 percent; social or community: 13.1 percent; sport, hobby, or arts: 3.5 percent. Religious organizations use volunteers 9.4 percent more than the closest organization type of educational institutions.

—United States Department of Labor Bureau of Labor Statistics

CEO's Perspective

"The overt objective in starting our volunteer program was to save our administrative costs," states Paul Calhoun, former CEO for an international mission organization. "Each year we saved well over $10,000 in salaries and benefits with our 50 volunteers. Side benefits, often unanticipated, were many. The morale of the whole salaried home office was hugely impacted, for it reinforced the sense of not just doing a job but of working together in the common cause to advance the kingdom of God. Though immeasurable, I believe the work efficiency of the whole staff rose by the example of the willing, enthusiastic volunteer team. The volunteers encouraged us by their interest and wholehearted support."

In addition, volunteers were motivated to give financially as they saw themselves drawn close to an organization in which they had ownership. They also became ambassadors, spreading the word to the community of its effectiveness.

Your Ambassador

Whether or not you embrace the concept, the individual volunteers and staff within your organization represent your agency to the world. By incorporating this model of ambassadors for the benefit of the organization, you will dynamically increase the effectiveness of the organization's mission, the quantity of dollars raised, the standing of your organization in the community, and the number of your volunteers.

Ways to increase ambassadorship of staff and volunteers

Give them an identity. Early in my time at a mission organization, my direct superior, Leo H. Cullum, requested I implement nametags for volunteers. Since there were only five volunteers at the time, I thought he was crazy and offered to personally introduce him to each of them. Leo saw the bigger picture, though. The nametags helped us determine which workers were paid and which were volunteers, and as the number of volunteers grew, the nametags served as an added security measure for our organization.

Another step toward creating an identity was accomplished by providing red polo shirts with the organization's name and logo on them. A shirt was given to each volunteer who agreed to come back after the first time of service. An unexpected bonus from the shirts was that the volunteers became walking billboards.

We provided polo shirts, because in our organization a large number of the volunteers were older women who didn't want to wear T-shirts. However, a T-shirt or ball cap can work just as well. It can be anything that sets your group apart and establishes the individuals who wear it as part of your team.

The value of statements made about your organization from a volunteer is much higher than by paid staff. Other volunteers come to the organization by the excitement, commitment, and encouragement of volunteers. Donors often become volunteers. The importance of volunteers cannot be overstated. —Leo H. Cullum

Educate them. At an international nonprofit organization where I worked, we wanted our volunteers telling the organization's stories out in the community. While their red shirts and other promotional clothing were often conversation-starters, volunteers needed to be prepared to tell the stories about our work in developing countries. The best way to accomplish this education was to ask missionary staff members returning from overseas to take time to talk to the volunteers. We formalized this arrangement by setting up a scheduled time each week to coincide with the time the largest group of volunteers was working.

These in-service meetings lasted about twenty minutes and were scheduled during the volunteers' break time. In this way, the volunteers received the "insider" information, often being the first to hear the field stories and view the newest photos. This knowledge added importance to their status as volunteers and excitement as they saw the end result of their labor. They spread this contagious passion into the marketplace as they told the organization's story.

I have been told many times that these weekly events were among the key reasons the volunteers kept coming back. The firsthand information added passion and ownership to their tasks. They saw and understood that what they were doing had a direct effect on the world and the work being done in the field by the missionaries.

Case in point: Lee and Ilene Morrow had been married for more than eighteen years. Lee had worked proudly for twelve years with the New York Fire Department until he was injured and had to retire. Lee began a new career working in accounting for the federal government. When both Lee and Ilene retired, they became faithful weekly volunteers and were asked to join the volunteer team of an international office of a nonprofit organization.

Lee spent his time volunteering in the accounting department, and Ilene worked in the international office. One morning a visiting missionary was sharing photos of picture books being used in a foreign country. The books taught important health concepts and Christian principles to illiterate nationals. Ilene was overwhelmed and in tears when she saw the photos of the picture books. Her volunteer task had been to copy and fold those very picture books!

Here was the work of her hands—those picture books impacting the world for Christ in a faraway place she would never visit. She remarked later, "It was a most beautiful thing to see the little books I had been putting together being used for the prevention of disease and also telling the salvation story, the love of Jesus."

The estimated dollar value of volunteer time was $19.51 per hour in 2007. There are a few states that have a higher rate: District of Columbia, $30.10; New York: $26.18; Massachusetts, $24.29; and California, $21.97.
—*Independent Sector*[1]

Ken Burton, a volunteer who stuffed envelopes with letters to donors requesting prayer and financial support, commented, "I personally liked to hear from the missionaries. After we sent out the letters, I often wondered what was actually happening on the field. The missionaries gave a personal account of what the letters to the donors meant. They connected what we were doing in the mailroom with what the crews were doing in the field."

Lowell Andrews shares, "A question-and-answer session with the missionaries opens up things you will normally not hear or read about in their newsletters. Hearing from the missionaries brings a deep inner satisfaction to the results of our work and a special closeness to each of the missionaries."

We have 200 volunteers a year collaborating in several projects. They help in outreach, communication, the magazine, fundraising, researching, and so on. They contribute by keeping alive projects that staff members cannot do by themselves; they promote the mission of the organization and become our ambassadors worldwide.
—*Carolina Villanueva, Manager of Intern and Volunteer Department,*
Idealistas.org, Buenos Aires

Give gifts with a purpose. In a future chapter I'll give ways to show appreciation to your volunteers, but I want to touch on just one way that applies here, which can be summed up in one word: gifts—not just any gifts, but gifts with a purpose. By the word *purpose* I mean the gifts have multiple functions. One is to thank the volunteers, but the second is just as important—if not more so.

The second function is advertisement. Every gift given from the organization to volunteers should carry the organization's logo and name. *Shameless marketing,* you may be thinking. Perhaps, but let me add that your organization is paying for the items. As an example, we gave the volunteers umbrellas one year. They were good-quality, collapsible, useful items. They were red, the mission's signature color, and the organization's logo was printed along with the organization's name in large, easy-to-read white letters. Opened on a rainy day, our volunteers became instant ambassadors. That is just one example, but every item an organization pays for should include at least the organization's logo and, if there's space, the name of the organization and contact information.

Use printed materials effectively. Clear and easy-to-follow printed materials with great photos are a necessity. In my view, one of the biggest mistakes an organization can make is trying to tell its whole story in one brochure. My mantra is always "Leave them asking for more." The point of any type of printed materials, including brochures and newsletters, is to get the person to ask the next question. Your primary goal is to engage readers and hook their interest, leaving them wanting to know more.

The printed materials should also be readily available, placed in a centrally located information rack or a storage area accessible at all times to volunteers and staff members. The aim is to get your organization's materials into the hands of those who can benefit your organization, thus enabling anyone to be an emissary for you.

By way of example, Lowell Andrews and his wife, Phyllis, travel yearly to a recreational vehicle campground in the southern portion of our state. They take along a handful of brochures about the organization to hand out to those they meet. They have also had opportunities to talk about the organization during church services held at the campground.

1930s: At the height of the Great Depression, United States President Franklin D. Roosevelt established the Civilian Conservation Corps (CCC) as a way to put idle hands to productive use to meet public needs. From 1933 to 1942, the CCC put some three million unemployed people to work clearing trails and restoring public lands. They have been credited with renewing the nation's decimated forests by planting an estimated three billion trees. And more than 40,000 illiterates were taught to read and write through the education component of the corps.

—*National & Community Service—Government Support for Volunteering*

Thank them. You can never thank volunteers enough. They're giving up their time and expending their energy on behalf of your organization. Thank them sincerely and often!

Volunteers contribute in ways that go beyond helping with your workload. Through them you have the possibility of touching lives, sharing your organization's story, and truly impacting your community and world.

Recap

- Volunteers contribute by performing more tasks than you may have previously imagined.
- You also impact the lives of your volunteers in numerous ways.
- Volunteers provide a tax break for your organization.
- Volunteers represent your organization to the world.

> *Volunteers contribute in every aspect of our operation. We have over 400 regular volunteers that provide service to our organization on an ongoing basis. Some work one or two days a year, while others work full-time.*
> —Anita Hellam, Habitat for Humanity

WHERE AND HOW DO YOU FIND VOLUNTEERS?

Throughout my life, I've seen the difference that volunteering efforts can make in people's lives. I know the personal value of service as a local volunteer.
—Jimmy Carter

Finding volunteers can seem like an overwhelming task. A good place to start is to determine what kind of volunteer would be a good fit for your organization. This can be accomplished by referring to the Department of Labor task breakdown at the beginning of the previous chapter. Find your category to discover who the typical persons volunteering in that category might be. Once you know who they are, you can begin to look for them. But let's step back and take this to a higher plain and see first what God has to say about volunteers and where to find them.

You see your calling, brethren, that not many wise according to the flesh, not many mighty, not many noble, are called. But God has chosen the foolish things of the world to put to shame the wise, and God has chosen the weak things of the world to put to shame the things which are mighty . . . that no flesh should glory in His presence . . . that, as it is written, "He who glories, let him glory in the LORD" (1 *Corinthians* 1:26-27, 29, 31).

These verses eloquently place us all on the same level in God's eyes. Rank, means, strength, and intelligence are not the standards God uses for those He calls to service. Verse 31 emphasizes the main point of the passage by stating clearly that God is to receive the glory. As 1 Corinthians tells us, anyone can be the one God is going to use to bring Him glory. Widen your perspective, and look at people through different eyes.

First Things First

In order to find a volunteer, you must know your need. Below are a few questions that will help you establish your focus and narrow your search for the volunteers God wants for your organization. Please don't skip this exercise. The information gleaned will be the foundation on which your volunteer program is built. If problems arise along the way, they can almost always be traced back to the lack of forethought invested in planning the volunteer program. Taking a few minutes now will set you on a firm footing.

Focus Questions

1. What has brought you to the point of desiring to learn more about volunteers and developing a volunteer program?

2. What have been your personal experiences as a volunteer?

3. Are you alone in the move to use volunteers within your organization?

4. If the answer to question three is no, then who are your supporters?

5. If the answer to question three is yes, then do you have someone to turn to for prayer support? This will be essential for your success. Who could be that support person? He or she could be within the organization or outside it.

6. What discussions have taken place with the whole staff about using volunteers?

7. Do you have any volunteers working with you now? If yes, how many?

8. Where did these volunteers come from? How were they recruited?

9. How long have they been with the organization?

10. What is your biggest concern about using volunteers?

Now that you've taken a few minutes to write your answers to the focus questions, let's break the questions down one by one.

What has brought you to the point of desiring to learn more about volunteers and developing a volunteer program?

You're probably reading this book because you and your organization have a need. Most likely there's too much work and too little money to hire additional staff. While you may see this situation as a problem, the reality is that you're on the brink of discovering something great.

What has been your personal experience as a volunteer?

If your own volunteer experience was unpleasant, you might be leery of repeating it with others. Hopefully it was rewarding and will stand as an encouragement to move you forward. Regardless of what your circumstances were, here's your chance to create a new and beneficial opportunity for others and to impact the effectiveness of your organization as well.

Are you alone in the move to use volunteers within your organization?

These next three focus questions tackle a very important point that must be in place before you start or restart a volunteer program. Do you have someone supporting you as you move forward with this project? You need to enlist the support of a trusted person who will stand with you during this process and act as a prayer partner and, if necessary, a sounding board. If you don't have anyone within your organization to fill this essential role, look elsewhere, and ask someone you trust. It's vital for success.

Pray about who this person should be. Formalize the arrangement by asking the person to pray about the matter, telling the individual how important he or she will be to the success of the project and asking for a one-year commitment. Consistent communication with your prayer partner can be maintained through a shared list of prayer needs for your project. You can convey your requests via e-mail, meeting over coffee weekly, or in whatever other way works best for both of you. This should not be a one-way prayer support relationship. Your support person should have the opportunity to include his or her own prayer needs on the list. Your record of answered prayers will also provide a wonderful platform of praise.

What discussions have taken place with the whole staff about using volunteers?

Whether your organization has a staff of two or two hundred, the staff can be your biggest hindrance or strongest building block in developing a flourishing volunteer ministry. Chapter four will cover this in detail. Suffice it to say that it's imperative to get the staff behind this project from the outset.

Do you have volunteers working with you now? Where did they come from, and how long have they been with the organization?

If you have volunteers already, your next step is to meet with each one individually. If you have only one, this will be a simple task.

During these informal meetings you'll want to do a lot of listening. Yes—listening! Begin by thanking them for the time they've invested in volunteering, and then ask them for their perception on how things are working. Ask for permission to take notes during the meeting, and let them know that the reason for doing so is to help you remember the important things they're going to say.

Next, ask them what they like about volunteering. Take notes. Then ask them what they would like to see changed. Reassure them that their answers are going to benefit the whole organization and that what they have to say is important to you. Encourage them to honestly express their opinions and share their perspectives. You may need to ask this question again in different ways to get more information. If there's a problem in your current program, this is the person who can help you. Remember to listen; don't defend. Giving volunteers permission to honestly express their concerns is paramount if you want the program to move forward. Toward the end of your time together, ask if they would be willing to invite friends or relatives to come in and volunteer.

We actively recruit volunteers. We know what jobs must be filled, and we contact people who have the appropriate skills, inviting them to consider working on our team. Some volunteers come to us unsolicited. That's a benefit of being part of an organization that has a reputation for working with volunteers. Our volunteer coordinator frequently speaks to clubs, groups, churches, and organizations to get people fired up about how we're changing lives.

—Anita Hellam, Habitat for Humanity

Your current volunteers can be your biggest source of additional volunteers. The exception to this is if they perceive problems have gone unattended. If you address the problems, you'll provide hope to the volunteers. If you have problems, perceived or real, you're not ready to expand your volunteer program. Deal with the problems before you attempt to move forward. If your volunteers are happy, appreciated, and feel as if their input is valued, they'll be your biggest advocates to bring in more people. Word of mouth is your best advertising tool. Even if you put fliers in the bulletin, ads in the newspaper, or speak before Sunday School classes or social groups, it's what the current volunteers say that matters most. Take one of them with you if you're given the opportunity to present the need to a group. Let the volunteers tell about their personal experiences.

Gang of Five

There were five volunteers with the mission organization the first year I started working there. One was Lowell, the husband of the receptionist, Phyllis Andrews, who had previously worked with the mission organization's CEO, Paul Calhoun, at his prior business. The other four volunteers were Leah Wilson, Marti Petersen, and two close friends, Arvilla and Helen Foss. All these individuals were in their late sixties or early seventies. What I discovered after spending time talking to each of them individually was that each was completely committed to the purpose of the organization. They loved the CEO, loved what the organization stood for, and were committed to helping. It was interesting to me that their expressed concern was that they wanted more work.

After the problems voiced by the volunteers were resolved, the number of volunteers began to increase. Staff members invited family and friends to join in. The volunteers spread the word among their friends and family. The program began to expand exponentially, and we reached the point where people were calling and walking in off the street to ask about volunteering. Although that situation is desirable, it's one that can create problems if the organization is not prepared for the growth. The program needs to be in place with a strong leadership team ready to handle a large influx of volunteers.

In the beginning you may be begging for volunteers, but if your program is sound, offers real tasks through which people can get involved with the organization, is encouraging and appreciative of the volunteers, and you're praying—your volunteer program will grow.

What is your biggest concern about using volunteers?

You may be thinking, *I'll never find even one volunteer!* If you currently do not have a single volunteer, enlist a good friend. Ask him or her to come in for one hour a week. Make the experience enjoyable and, positive, and show your appreciation. Don't go on and on about how bad things are, how overworked everyone is, and how unfair it is that there are no volunteers to help. Take the high road. Your friend may or may not become a long-term volunteer, but he or she can help you get things moving. If your friend has a great time volunteering, he or she will tell someone else. If you don't have a friend you feel you can ask, ask a relative. Ask that person to volunteer for a specific time period—maybe two months—or for a specific task. Tell the friend or relative that you would like for him or her to evaluate the experience and give you input about what he or she feels is working or areas that need improvement.

One Is a Beginning

At a small church where I worked in southern California, I was the only administrative staff person in the church office. While the majority of my job involved working for the senior pastor, I also assisted the high school, junior high, and children's department directors, along with the associate pastor and the church board.

Because I had moved to the area to work for the senior pastor at his request, I didn't know anyone when I moved there. It took time to get involved in the church and figure out who might be willing to lend me a hand. The workload was overwhelming. In addition to the usual responsibilities, the job included a considerable amount of time at the photocopy machine reproducing Sunday School materials, the weekly bulletins, congregational mailings, as well as providing for event set-up and coordination. Along with persistent prayer, I began to keep a record of the work I could hand over to a volunteer if I had one. The list grew longer and longer.

Not surprisingly, God delivered. Diane Bahruth and her husband had been church members for quite some time. She and I hit it off the first time we met. Diane had not worked outside the home while raising her children. After taking her out to lunch several times, I discovered that she was at a place in her life in which she was looking at options for expanding her role outside the home. That was an open door, and I jumped right through it. I assured her that she could just try it for a period of time to see if she liked it and that if it was working out well for both of us, she could become a volunteer.

Depending on the size and age of the organization, you find them on the outer or inner perimeters of the agency. Often they're looking for ways to become involved. It's the responsibility of leadership and paid staff to keep a watchful eye on suspects, prospects, donors, and friends of the agency or cause. Volunteers are an extension of the nonprofit to the community.

—*Leo H. Cullum*

By faith I had already prepared for Diane's arrival long before I knew who she was. I had a list of tasks, so she was able to start contributing immediately. The first day we planned that she would come to the office in the morning around 10:30 and work for an hour. Afterward, over lunch, I asked questions to find out what she thought about her first experience. She told me she felt valuable, excited, and enthusiastic. Over time, she was able to expand her volunteer hours to a regular weekly schedule.

Diane became so valuable to the staff and to me that she was eventually hired to work part-time. It was a great confirmation to her of her valuable skills. She eventually went on to a full-time job at a large university, where she's now an executive assistant.

Where Do You Find Volunteers?

- *Select a prayer partner.* Ask God to direct you to the person with whom He wants you to establish a prayer partnership. This one action has the power to determine the success of your program.
- *Start with the ones you have.* Listen to the volunteers you already have, even if there are only a few or even just one. Hear what problems they feel need to be addressed to make the program grow. Then do it! These individuals can be

your greatest source of future volunteers. You're starting over fresh with this group that God has gathered together. You're beginning a new day. Make sure to communicate this important point to them.

- *Ask a friend or family member.* If you don't have any volunteers, you have to start somewhere. The best place to start is with someone you know. Try asking a friend or family member. Ideally, that person will enjoy the experience so much that he or she will sign on for a longer-term commitment.
- *Take a volunteer with you.* If you offer or are asked to speak to a group such as an adult Sunday School class or a social group, take one of your satisfied volunteers along with you to share his or her story of volunteering. The personal story from the volunteer will do more than you ever could in motivating people to join.
- *Be sure to have volunteer recruitment handouts available that contain contact information, volunteer hours, and tasks to be done.* This can be in the form of a simple business card, a sheet of paper, or a brochure. Be sure to have lots of handouts so they're always available. Staff members and current volunteers can leave them in medical and dental offices, business offices, senior centers, and so on. If you're with a mission or non-profit organization, ask local churches if you can provide handouts to be placed in a display rack, pinned on a bulletin board, handed out as fliers tucked in the church bulletin, or left at an information desk.

Don't forget to recruit online. Post needs on your own Web site, and keep them current. Remember to include contact information. Check out the following Web sites:

- *VolunteerMatch,* <www.volunteermatch.org>. Since 1998 VolunteerMatch has been the Web's largest and most popular United States-based volunteer network with tens of thousands of active volunteer opportunities from more than 62,000 participating nonprofit organizations.

- ChristianVolunteering.org, <www.ChristianVolunteering.org>, matches volunteers to volunteer opportunities and helps organizations recruit volunteers through online volunteer matching. In many ways ChristianVolunteering.org is like job matching Web sites like Monster.com, except that it matches volunteers to organizations with volunteer opportunities. Organizations can post volunteer opportunities to recruit volunteers online.
- 1-800-Volunteer.org, <www.1-800-Volunteer.org>, is a national database of volunteer opportunities powered by a volunteer management system for nonprofits.
- CharityAmerica.com, <www.charityamerica.com>, registers nonprofit organizations for online donations and posts their volunteer opportunities.
- Network for Good, <www.networkforgood.org>, brings together many resources that make it easy to donate to any charity using Guidestar's database of charitable organizations and searches for volunteer opportunities using VolunteerMatch's database.
- ServeNet, <www.servenet.org>, focuses on volunteerism and community service, including a place to post volunteer opportunities.
- Volunteer Solutions, <www.volunteersolutions.org>, helps volunteers, nonprofit agencies, corporations, event organizers, and volunteer centers get connected.

For churches: For a sermon series on service or spiritual gifts, ask for an appointment with the senior pastor to present the need for at least one sermon on service or spiritual gifts. During that appointment be prepared to present your needs, specifically listing the tasks for which volunteers would be useful. You should also present your training methods, what the cost would be for the church, and how you plan on recognizing the volunteers for their service. Preparation for this meeting is necessary in order to be successful. Put your information in a clear, easy-to-understand printed format to give to the pastor. Bullet points are usually an effective method to present your material.

- *Newspaper, bulletin, newsletters:* For churches, place an announcement of volunteer needs in the bulletin, on a bulletin board, and in brochures in the information rack. On these items it's important to ask for specific action steps such as filling out a pew/communication card, calling the office, and attending an information meeting. For nonprofit organizations, place an ad in the local newspaper. There are community interest sections in newspapers that sometimes allow for free placement of information. Ask to be included in citywide newsletters, church newsletters, and church bulletins with an attention-grabbing ad that requires a specific action step, as mentioned above.

- *Local newspaper article:* Contact your local newspaper's religious department via e-mail. In the e-mail provide a "hook" that will get them interested in writing a story about one or more of your volunteers. Don't try to get them to write about the entire program. Provide contact information to be included in the article or at the end of the article. Make a specific request to have this contact information included. Never assume the contact information will be included; it's important to ask.

- *Check with your local home-schooling network:* Home-schooling parents are looking for opportunities for their children to learn by hands-on experience. Your public school can connect you with your local network—usually through e-mail.

- *Local college placement center:* While the placement center is used to help students find jobs, there are also occasions when students might want to volunteer either in their area of study or future area of employment. Call the college nearest you, and ask the placement staff person if you could provide fliers, posters, or brochures.

1960s: The cause of federally supported civilian service was renewed with President John F. Kennedy's creation of the Peace Corps and President Lyndon B. Johnson's creation of VISTA (Volunteers in Service to America). In that same period, the Foster Grandparents, Senior Companions, and Retired Senior Volunteer Program began to show how older Americans could establish meaningful relationships with people in need.

—*National & Community Service—Government Support for Volunteering[1]*

Your volunteers are out there, and they desire and are waiting for an opportunity to serve

To Recap

- Pray!
- Start with one.
- Invite a friend or family member to volunteer for a short amount of time.
- Create a handout to give to key groups. Include the organization's needs and contact information.
- Use online sites.
- Promote service through sermon topics (for churches).
- Advertise.
- Pray again!

BEFORE VOLUNTEERS ARRIVE

Bite off more than you can chew; then chew it. Plan more than you can do; then do it.
—Anonymous

Before the first volunteer arrives, you must get your staff interested in using volunteers and involved in the process. Regardless of the size of the staff, everyone must be on board with this undertaking. If you are the only administrative staff member working for several people, each individual will need to be made aware of your reasons and plan for involving volunteers.

The same is true if you work for an organization with a large administrative staff. The approval of your immediate supervisor, and in some cases the head of the organization, will be essential. Why? You need as much support as possible. The endorsement from your president, senior pastor, and so on can be the key to making the endeavor successful. The best way to receive backing is to list the tasks for which you will use volunteers and show how this will save the organization time and money. This can be easily demonstrated by calculating the hourly wage times the number of hours it would take you to complete all the tasks you have listed. Dream big! This list is your opportunity to help develop a vision for the future of your organization.

With a large staff, once you have your superior's approval, send an e-mail outlining what you have planned and why. If the executive you're dealing with is agreeable, have him or her send out the preliminary announcement containing a statement that you'll be sending more information shortly.

Here's a sample e-mail that you could send after the appropriate announcement has been made by the appropriate person.

Sample

From
Sent [date]
To all Staff
Subject: Volunteer Program
Attachment—Volunteer Request Form

Greetings!

By now you have received the e-mail announcing our new volunteer ministry. [If you already have one or more volunteers, then the statement would be "Announcing our newly revised/ inaugurated volunteer ministry."] We are excited about the possibilities volunteers will provide for [organization's name] to expand its vision and outreach.

Here is what we need from you:

- Your prayers for wisdom, direction, and information on how you will participate.
- A list of possible tasks to be performed for you by a volunteer.
- Days and times that would work best for you to have a volunteer working with you.
- Skills needed to complete the task(s) successfully.
- Your questions.

I have attached a Volunteer Request Form. A form will be needed for each one-time task. If you need a volunteer on a weekly basis, you will need to fill out the form only once. Please completely fill in only the top half of the form. It will be returned to you after a volunteer has been assigned to your task. The bottom half of the form is to be completed after the task has been accomplished.

This form can be found _____. [Make this form available on your computer network and in printed format in a centrally located place.]

The volunteer program will be included on the support staff meeting agenda on [date]. I look forward to your input at that time but would also welcome any questions you may have now. [A weekly or monthly support/administrative staff meeting is a valuable communication tool for your staff. If you do not already hold such meetings, I recommend you consider doing so. Beginning a volunteer program can be one of the first topics on the agenda.]

Thank you!

Sincerely yours,

 ————————————————————————

Our staff has grown to understand that a volunteer will be a valuable co-laborer. They appreciate the way their workloads can be lessened by properly training, engaging, and supervising another. When volunteers show up and demonstrate a lack of commitment, our leadership team has the authority to send that volunteer home. We frequently interview volunteers before accepting their services. There is no guarantee that everyone who volunteers will be a good fit.

—Anita Hellam, Habitat for Humanity

Volunteer Request Form Sample

The following is an example of a Volunteer Request Form I developed and used at one organization where I worked. This can serve as a starting point from which to create a form that would be effective for your organization. You are welcome to use it as it is, if you choose.

VOLUNTEER REQUEST FORM

Your Name _____ Today's Date _____

I need volunteer help _____

_____

_____

The best time for them to complete this task would be on _____
(Date)

between _____ and _____.
         (Time)   (Time)

Deadline _____ .

VOLUNTEER ASSIGNMENT

Volunteer(s) Assigned _____

Volunteer(s) Contacted on _____

They will be here on _____ at _____ .

They will report to _____ .

AFTER TASK IS COMPLETED

Was the task completed to your satisfaction? _____ Comments: _____

_____

_____

Did you remind the volunteer to sign the "Volunteer Book"? Our auditor requires it. _____

The last section of the form is to be completed by the staff member to whom the volunteer reported. The staff member's input is valuable to ensure that things are running smoothly. If any issues were brought up on the forms, they should be addressed as soon as possible.

Staff Responses

This announcement is going to elicit many different feelings and responses among your staff. These responses tend to break down into the following categories:

- I don't know how to work with a volunteer.

- It would take me more time to show someone how to do the job than to just do it myself.
- I'm afraid that if I train someone to do some of my tasks, the volunteer will take my job. (This concern may be present but unexpressed. It should be discussed and handled with sensitivity.)

Any one of these points has the potential to derail a volunteer program. Let's address them one by one.

I don't know how to work with a volunteer. This excuse can easily be dealt with by sitting down with the staff member and walking through the process with him or her. It's often just a lack of instruction or information that creates this fear. With knowledge and reassurance it can generally be overcome.

Assure the staff member that you'll be available for questions that may come up. Also remind the staff member that this relationship is primarily a friendship he or she will establish with the volunteer. That knowledge should take some of the edge off. The volunteer wants to feel valued and appreciated, just as the staff member does. Ask the staff member to imagine being in the volunteer's shoes. The volunteer may in many ways be more unnerved by this experience than the staff member is.

It would take me more time to show someone how to do the job than to just do it myself. This defense often comes from the staff member's inability to see the big picture. Sit down with the staff member, and ask about his or her daily workload. Inquire about the mundane or what he or she considers the boring parts of the job. Let him or her talk, and once a list of tasks has been determined, help the staff member see that these are the very kinds of jobs a volunteer could complete and take off the staff member's to-do list. Once the volunteer is able to handle these tasks, the staff member will be freed up to care for the jobs there's never enough time for. It will take some up-front training time for the staff member and the volunteer, but the rewards in easing the ongoing workload will be undeniable.

I used to keep a tray of work on a shelf next to my desk. I put anything on that tray that needed to be done but didn't need immediate attention. It often included filing, items to be posted on the master calendar, report reviews, data input, and so on. The tray was sometimes piled two feet high. When a staff member was struggling with the idea of taking time to train a volunteer versus doing it himself or herself, I showed the person my pile, which wasn't generally visible to guests who came to my office. I described how I would take the bottom few inches from the pile and give it to a volunteer, explaining that handing off even this much would relieve my workload and stress level. I taught my volunteers to come into the office and go directly to the pile. In even one hour a week, the impact on the size of that pile was unbelievable.

The visual aid of the diminishing pile of volunteer tasks was usually very effective in convincing the reluctant staff member. But if this explanation still wasn't enough to convince him or her, I would ask the staff member to consider that this might be a way that God was trying to work in the volunteer's life.

Bernice Norris was employed in the finance department of a mission organization. Her perspective as an employee:

I really looked forward to having Helen Foss and Marti Petersen come in and help with the filing. I don't like to file, but more importantly, it was a joy to hear to them giggling and bantering, asking me to settle disagreements on how something should be filed. With all the goings-on to get the job done, it was the absolute devotion and caring they showed for each other—Christian caring, that is—that touched my heart.

The same was true of sweet little Lee Morrow. He would come in just bursting to tell a silly joke before beginning his assignment and then work quietly for the remainder of the morning.

I don't know how to put into words how true Christian caring comes across without specific words being spoken, but it does.

After retiring from her position in the financial department, Bernice volunteered at the same organization. Here is Bernice's input from the volunteer perspective.

To have a group of people come together to do some task for the good of the organization is great, but what the volunteer receives spiritually is beyond words. It means so much to know the group cares if you show up or not and that at break time or quitting time prayers will be offered for the organization as well as for individuals. Once again, it's a God thing. I can't explain it.

Sarah (not her real name) didn't speak often, and when she did, it was just a little above a whisper. The first time she showed up, she came to the volunteer workroom and, almost unnoticed, stood against the wall. But she was noticed, because she wasn't the first to display shyness in this manner. Someone immediately introduced herself to Sarah and took her to meet one of the leadership members. The leadership team was made up of couples, and one of the wives reached out and took Sarah's hand. She showed her where the restrooms were located and where to get a cup of coffee and gave her a short tour of the facilities. By the end of the work time, Sarah was smiling. She returned faithfully to help a few times each week for a long time.

Once during a staff meeting I was informed there was a volunteer who wasn't doing tasks correctly. When I asked who it was, the name given was Sarah, so I asked what seemed to be the problem. The response from the staff member seemed frivolous, so my next question was directed at her. "Okay," I asked, "tell me what you've done to help her."

The question stopped the staff member in her tracks. I then told all of the staff present that the reason we had volunteers wasn't just to get our work done. I pointed out that we had been granted the privilege from God of having a role in the volunteer's life. I shared some of Sarah's situation with them—that she had only one family member she seldom saw who was living in another state. Sarah had read the notice about the organization's need for volunteers in her church bulletin, and it had taken her months to work up the courage to come to the mission office. She was frightened, uncomfortable, and very uncertain about what she was doing. What she encountered from the moment she opened the front door of the office was love and a sense of family. For the first time in a very long time, she felt included. Sarah didn't know we had prayed for her and all the other volunteers long before they ever arrived. Gratefully, the staff members got the point of befriending Sarah and began to go out of their way to reach out to our other volunteers.

I'm afraid that if I train someone to do some of my tasks, the volunteer will take my job. This is the hardest staff objection to overcome, because it is often not expressed. That's why you will need to introduce the fear during your support staff meeting. In fact, all three of these possible staff responses should be addressed at this first staff meeting about volunteers.

With regard to the fear of a staff member losing his or her job to a volunteer, let's approach it from a different viewpoint. Consider the experience of Linda Raymer, a former human resources manager at a nonprofit organization;

One thing I learned about volunteers when I worked with them is not to treat them as employees. Actually I learned that from watching a fellow employee mishandle volunteers. He had the mentality that volunteers could and should be used in much the same way as an employee. I tried to tell him that volunteers generally come at the job with a different mind-set, many of them retired from a job and not wanting to take on another. They want to help out, not be saddled with lots of job responsibility that pays nothing. I think employees are somewhat nurtured by their paycheck, which is not to say they don't want other things from their employment; however, volunteers do not get monetary compensation and are generally nurtured by interaction with others and a perception of meaningful contribution.

Volunteers are not employees, and employees are not volunteers. It is a major distinction that needs to be stated and reinforced frequently.

Another way to look at this is from Diane's standpoint. Her story is included in chapter two. Diane had not been employed outside her home for many years. She had been hard at work raising her children. After being away from the workplace for a long time, she found that her confidence level was low, and she needed a safe environment to make mistakes and learn from them and to gain experience. Once she was comfortable and confident, I pushed to get her a paid staff position at the church. Her job lasted for less than a year, however, because she soon felt strong enough in her own abilities to apply for a better-paying job at a university. You might be thinking that I put in the time to train Diane only for her to leave when a better opportunity became available.

In a way, you would be correct. It has happened to me on several occasions, and a number of people I know who work with volunteers have had this happen to them also. But remember that this is a ministry that works both ways. The needs of each volunteer are unique, and whatever role God calls us to play in his or her life is significant and worthwhile.

To answer the original question directly, I have never known of a single case in which someone has lost his or her job because a volunteer was doing the work better and the organization decided to fire the staff member and keep the volunteer. The reality is that the volunteer won't do your all-encompassing job. The volunteer's role is to handle specific projects or portions of the workload.

The staff is on board, and you have volunteers willing to come and help. Now what?

The staff and your superiors are on board. The staff members want to use volunteers and have turned in their forms with their projects listed. You know what the needs are and what timeframe will work best for the staff. During your preliminary meeting with the staff you went over the three major points of objection and calmed their fears. You've helped the staff understand that this is a two-way relationship; the volunteers are not intended to be personal servants but rather valued members of the team seeking to help accomplish the organization's goals.

We get many calls from human resource people asking for references for our volunteers, and we're happy to help them and provide accurate feedback on how they work. This has helped the volunteers to grow in the nonprofit sector and get good jobs. Volunteers see us as a way to get professional experience while helping others.

Our former volunteers also continue helping in other projects. We have a former volunteer helping in our upcoming event in Ecuador. Volunteers get us good contacts. We met with Google and started doing workshops because a volunteer helped us get connected.

—*Carolina Villanueva, Manager, Intern and Volunteer Department,*
Idealistas.org, Buenos Aires

Volunteers have been located and are interested in coming in and helping out. The date is set. What's next?

- All supplies, materials, equipment, tools, information, and other necessary items for the volunteers to complete their projects must be ready for them *before* they arrive. The most frequent complaint I hear is that the staff member wasn't ready for the volunteer, and the volunteer had to wait to get started on the assignment. Since the volunteer has only a certain window of time available, this lack of preparation squanders it.
- Set aside a place for volunteers to perform the needed task. If a computer is necessary, then a computer must be assigned, set up, and waiting. If table space is needed, have a space cleared and ready for the volunteer. The second most

common complaint I hear from volunteers is that there was no space assigned for them to work. The message this sends the volunteer is that he or she is too insignificant to warrant adequate preparation. Check with the human resources department to find out if there are rules or procedures the volunteers must abide by. If possible, ask someone in the human resources department to provide copies of the rules to hand out to the volunteers. This could entail things as simple as where the volunteer should park, what to do with personal belongings, break-time procedures (some companies do not use Styrofoam cups, only mugs; or there might be a cost for coffee). There may be policies regarding sexual harassment, procedures for filing grievances, and so on. There may also be confidentiality agreements, legal issues, or insurance restrictions that should be addressed. It's a good idea to find out what the requirements and concerns of the human resources department are before the volunteers arrive.

- Nametags are useful. When nametags were introduced at one organization where I worked, the staff thought we were crazy, since we only had five volunteers and everyone knew them. I reminded them the volunteer ministry was going to grow and someday they wouldn't know all of the volunteers' names. The staff was also encouraged to assume the responsibility and privilege of greeting and thanking the volunteers they spotted wearing nametags. This practice creates a wonderful attitude of gratitude.

The staff is on board and prepared. The staff understands the value of volunteers and the need to appreciate them. Tasks have been lined up, and the volunteers are scheduled to arrive.

To Recap

- The staff must be on board with this project!
- Address staff concerns specifically.

- Establish a list of tasks to be accomplished by volunteers.
- Take the steps necessary to be ready for the volunteers before they arrive, such as providing materials, space, nametags, and so on.

5 HOW TO KEEP VOLUNTEERS COMING BACK AFTER THE FIRST DAY

If you want to lift yourself up, lift up someone else.
—Booker T. Washington

In the early stages of your volunteer program, you'll probably be the volunteers' first contact. This is especially true with a small staff. You'll be the person who helps volunteers get acclimated for this new journey. With a larger administrative staff, and as the volunteer staff grows, the new volunteers' first contact will be with the volunteer coordinator. Even with a volunteer coordinator, the activities for the volunteers' first day will be the same.

Sarah's story in the last chapter is a wonderful example of how a new volunteer should be welcomed into your organization. When Sarah first came to volunteer, the volunteer staff consisted of more than fifty individuals. Not all of them work on the same days, but on Sarah's first day there were about eighteen volunteers working throughout the building with the majority working on a mailing task in the conference room.

Take the first step in faith. You don't have to see the whole staircase; just take the first step.

—*Martin Luther King Jr.*

Because Sarah walked into a well-established volunteer program, the receptionist knew exactly what to do. She greeted her, made a nametag for her, and then directed her to the conference room. When Sarah tentatively slipped into the conference room, the volunteer nearest the door greeted her and took her to meet Phyllis, the female half of the volunteer leadership couple. Phyllis showed Sarah where to put her purse, where the restrooms were located, how to find the coffee, and then gave her a quick tour of the facilities.

Phyllis introduced Sarah to Lowell, Phyllis's husband, who gave Sarah a questionnaire to fill out. Lowell then showed her what job the volunteers were working on that day. It happened to be a large mailing that involved stuffing materials into business size mailing envelopes. Sarah took to the task quickly. Lowell and Phyllis checked back with her often to make sure she was doing well and didn't need anything. She was also sitting between two other ladies, veterans of the volunteer program, and they kept an eye on her and were happy to answer her questions.

Sarah stayed for two-and-a-half hours and emptied her plastic mailing tub of envelopes. Phyllis talked with her before she left to find out if she had any concerns and to ask if she was interested in returning. Sarah was eager to return, and she was scheduled for the same day and time the following week.

Let's walk through a typical first day in a situation in which there are just a few volunteers and you're their first contact.

Here's a typical first day, step by step:

- The volunteer arrives at the scheduled time. If your organization has a receptionist, the receptionist should be made aware that a volunteer is scheduled to arrive and the time he or she is expected. You've asked the receptionist to alert you as soon as the volunteer arrives.

- When notified of the volunteer's arrival, you greet the volunteer, whom you've previously talked to on the telephone, and introduce yourself.

- Next, you take the volunteer on a short tour of the facility, which will include restroom locations, where to get coffee or soft drinks, where supplies are stored, the location where he or she will be working, and you'll include directions for how to find you—especially if the volunteer will not be working close to you. If the volunteer will be working with another staff member, introductions should be made.

- Once the tour is completed, you and the new volunteer should either return to your work area or to a private space so you can talk with the volunteer briefly. Answer any questions the volunteer has, and ask him or her to fill out a short volunteer questionnaire. The questionnaire is a valuable tool to discover hidden skills and where the volunteer's interests lie. From experience, Phyllis says, "Some volunteers are well-educated and have many abilities. They need to be used where they can best serve. Some volunteers do want to contribute in their skill area, but others don't want to do the same work they've done in the past. I was a receptionist and secretary for more than twenty years, and I no longer want to answer the phone." A questionnaire will help you determine what the volunteer wishes to gain from volunteer service and gives you an idea of his or her past experience and unique set of skills and interests. The questionnaire is kept on file, and a copy goes to the staff person with whom the volunteer will be working. The questionnaire itself is a simple form containing basic information. A full-size sample version of this form is located in chapter ten.

Questionnaire

Last Name _____ First Name _____

Phone number _____ Best time to call _____

Address _____

City, State _____ Zip _____

Birth date: (year not required) _____

Hobbies:

Spiritual Gifts:

Special training/experience:

Work experience:

Days & Time Available: (Check as many as apply)
Days—( ) Monday   ( ) Tuesday   ( ) Wednesday   ( ) Thursday   ( ) Friday
Time _____   _____   _____   _____   _____

Area of interest: (Check as many as apply. If you have any questions about what is involved with any of the areas, please feel free to ask)

Miscellaneous	Office	Software Experience
( ) Group work	( ) Computer work	( ) Word
( ) Working individually	( ) Filing	( ) Excel
( ) Research work	( ) Proofreading	( ) Photoshop (version ___)
( ) Driving to & from airport	( ) Copy work	( ) MS Outlook
___ Modesto	( ) Telephoning	( ) PageMaker (version ___)
___ San Francisco	( ) Fill in on phones	( ) PowerPoint
___ Sacramento	( ) Clerical support	( ) _____
( ) Housing visitors	( ) Bulk mailing work	
( ) Accounting interest	( ) Photo scanning	
( ) Fundraising interest	( ) _____	
( ) Fix-it person		
( ) Set up/take down for events		

( ) Other _____

Comments: (Please use the back of this sheet)

The "area of interest" section in the volunteer questionnaire was compiled from lists contributed by staff members for tasks they wished to have accomplished. The birth date information is included since it enables the organization to send a birthday card to the volunteer each year.

- When the questionnaire is completed and the volunteer's questions have been answered, personally walk the volunteer to the staff member who will be explaining the tasks he or she will be working on.

- Keep in mind that before the volunteer arrives, you will have checked with your staff member to make sure he or she is prepared and ready to show the volunteer what volunteer task he or she will be doing, a work space will be ready, and necessary equipment and needed supplies will be waiting.

- After the staff members have introduced themselves, the first order of business is to thank the volunteer for coming in to help.

- Next, a staff member will show the volunteer what tasks need to be completed and explain how they should be done. On the volunteer's first day, he or she may have lots of questions. Encourage the volunteer to ask questions. Questions are important and a good indication that the volunteer is interested and conscientious about the assigned task.

- When the volunteer has completed the task, the supervising staff member should review the completed job and respond to any questions that might have arisen. When finished, thank the volunteer for his or her work and express the hope that he or she will become a regular member of your organization's volunteer program.

- Ask the staff member to remind the volunteer to check in with you again before leaving. If the volunteer has forgotten where to find you, the staff member should accompany the volunteer to your office. This is your opportunity to follow up and find out how things went for the volunteer. Ask whether there are any problems that need to be addressed, and then find out if he or she is interested in returning. This is also a final opportunity to express your gratitude to the volunteer. This follow-up session does not need to take much time unless the volunteer indicates concerns or problems with the assignment. If so, you will want to spend additional time with the individual.

1990: United States President George H. W. Bush created the Commission on National and Community Service to administer grants to schools, to support service-learning in schools, higher education institutions, and community-based organizations and support full-time service across the nation.

—*National & Community Service—Government Support for Volunteering*[1]

After the volunteer has left, check in with the supervising staff member to get the completed Volunteer Request Form back, and ask for comments about how the volunteer completed the assigned task. If the staff member hasn't had time to fill out the appropriate portion of the form, take notes on the bottom section of the form as you talk with the staff member. Encourage the staff member to send the volunteer a thank-you note.

It's also a good idea for you to contact the volunteer again in the next few days. This contact allows you to see how he or she felt about the experience and if he or she is interested in returning. If this question was answered before the volunteer left the organization's office, then a thank-you note would be suitable. If the volunteer requested time to think and pray about returning, a telephone call after a suitable interval would be appropriate.

To Recap

- Volunteers are your invited guests and should be treated with respect, love, and care.
- Be prepared for their arrival.
- Take steps to make them feel welcome before, during, and after their visit with your organization.
- A questionnaire can be a key tool in guiding your volunteer program to success.

TRAINING VOLUNTEERS FOR SUCCESS

Any training that does not include the emotions, mind, and body is incomplete; knowledge fades without feeling.
—Anonymous

Success can depend on how well-prepared volunteers are to complete their assigned tasks. So spending time on the front end can save you a great deal of heartache, time, frustration, and conflict.

I Wanted to Help People, but I Didn't Know How.

I came to a point in life that I knew I wanted to help people, but I didn't know how. Then in my church bulletin I saw a request asking people to sign up if they felt God was calling them to help others by volunteering as a Stephen Minister. I knew this was my answer.

As a volunteer in this ministry, you frequently come alongside a person who is hurting, maybe from a terminal illness, divorce, grief, unemployment, depression, or a host of other reasons. Our role is not to tell them how to solve the problem but to be there for them to talk with—to be a good listener.

Thankfully, the Stephen Ministry has a great training program. It includes workbooks, several books, role playing, discussion groups, prayer, and supportive leadership. The training focuses on us as caregivers, teaching us how to deal with feelings; listen, establish and recognize boundaries; respect confidentiality; and identify and deal with mental health issues, including knowing when or if a person should be referred to a professional. The program also deals with training on how to serve those experiencing grief, depression, or getting a suicidal person the right help. We in no way take the place of a professional person who has more knowledge and education. We are there to listen and direct those in need to appropriate help when necessary. This training has given me a secure feeling about my ability to help others.

Because of the training, I'm confident that I can do this. I also know that the resources of the support group and Stephen Ministry leadership are available to help me through this assignment. Twice each month the caregivers meet as a support group for one another. We report how things are going, how we see our care relationship progressing, and we're able to ask questions and express concerns. Everything discussed during the support group meeting is confidential. The care recipient's name is never mentioned.

This whole experience has been so rewarding to me personally. Here I'm supposed to be the one helping and blessing someone else, but many times I feel that I'm the one getting the blessings (Laurie Freeman, Stephen Ministry volunteer).

Training is a key component in a successful volunteer program. Specific steps must be in place to ensure that volunteers are properly and thoroughly trained. One of the key methods for training, and I feel the most important one, is one-on-one interaction with a person who knows how to complete the task successfully. This could be another volunteer or a staff member.

However, in the early stages of the development of your volunteer program, that person will be the staff member in need of assistance.

The actual training methods will vary greatly, largely dependent upon the type and size of the organization. If your organization is medium to large, you'll need to work directly with and through Human Resources to comply with its requirements and training methods. If, however, your organization is smaller, the training methods will in all likelihood depend upon you alone.

We provide an orientation for our volunteers. We explain the mission and the various areas of service that could be appealing. We then ask them to complete an application to clarify their background and experience. When someone presents us with useful skills, he or she is referred to the appropriate team leader. Some of our regular volunteers have taken on the task of training and supervising new volunteers.

—*Anita Hellam, Habitat for Humanity*

There's no way to cover all the different kinds of training. There are, however, a few key characteristics that are essential to any successful training program, no matter the size of the program or the skills needed.

- *Respect:* Each volunteer comes to your organization as a gift and without exception should be treated with the utmost respect. I have had the pleasure of having my mom volunteer at one of the organizations I worked for, and it was extremely important to me that she be treated with respect. However, the way she was treated was the way I want every volunteer to be treated. Volunteers are there by choice. Out of the goodness of their hearts they are giving you an invaluable gift of time and service. Show regard and speak respectfully each time you come in contact with them. There are two concrete ways to show respect: **(1) Be ready for the volunteer before he or she arrives.** The volunteers should not be expected to sit and wait for you to print or copy the materials you want them to use. As a case in point: Ken and Jan Burton volunteered weekly at their church, folding and inserting the Sunday bulletins. As weeks went by, the materials frequently weren't ready when they arrived, and they were left to sit and wait. They politely expressed their displeasure at the waste of their time. The final straw was one week when they had waited over two hours. Jan complained to a friend who worked at another nonprofit ministry in the same town. The friend told Jan they needed volunteers and assured her that she and her husband would never have to wait for the work. As a result, Ken and Jan no longer fold and stuff bulletins. They have now been successfully serving at the other non-profit group for years and have even moved to a role on the volunteer leadership team. **(2) Have a dedicated place for the volunteer to work.** It doesn't have to be large or fancy—it just needs to exist. This one small gesture shows you care enough to prepare and that you value the service and the individual.

- *Responsibility:* Help your volunteers be successful by providing several methods of training. This could be verbal or written, taking the form of a demonstration or even a short video clip. Above all, provide an atmosphere where questions are welcomed and encouraged. The volunteers need to understand what's expected of them and feel comfortable asking questions.

- *Accountability:* Who do volunteers go to with questions or concerns? This should be made clear from the outset. Who will be reviewing their work to make sure it was completed well? Protect your volunteer, if you have one assigned to you specifically. In other words, if you have a volunteer you use on a regular basis, all his or her work should come through you and not another staff member.

This could be a very confusing situation for the volunteer. From the outset, it must be clear to whom he or she will answer. If you are in a one-person office, then, of course, you're the person he or she will report to, even if the task has come from a director or pastor. Your role is to serve as the volunteer's contact and to provide a consistent link of accountability.

Training and orientation should be provided to all volunteers and should include the background on the organization, how volunteers will help the organization to accomplish its mission, specific work tasks volunteers will perform, hours of work, responsibilities, scheduling, and encouragement to recruit. —*Leo H. Cullum*

Handbook

In order to be a bit more specific about training, it's important to have informational materials to give to all new volunteers to help them understand what's expected of them and what policies your organization has in place. Generally speaking, volunteering means that these individuals agree to perform their assigned duties to the best of their abilities and to remain loyal to the mission, goals, and procedures of the organization. A handbook helps define this concept and provides specific details about various assignments or tasks. The handbook may take the form of a few pages of eight-and-a-half-by-eleven paper folded in half, or it might be something along the lines of the organization's employee handbook. I've included a sample of a complete volunteer handbook in chapter 10—"Resources for Volunteers." To be a valuable resource, these materials should cover the following:

- The reasons we use volunteers, the purpose and mission of the organization, and the reasons for our guidelines
- Regular office hours and holiday schedules

- General guidelines:
  - Personal appearance
  - Office housekeeping
  - Telephone calls and office visits
  - Courtesy and conversation
  - Confidentiality
  - Concerns and problems
  - Sexual harassment
  - Job description for volunteers

Please feel free to use this as a guideline for your own use. The contents of this particular handbook went through a vigorous review process by several committees and departments, including the executive leadership committee of the organization, the human resource department, the volunteer leadership team, and various support staff.

1993: United States President Bill Clinton and Congress created the Corporation for National and Community Service by combining the Commission on National and Community Service with the federal domestic volunteer agency, ACTION, uniting the full range of domestic community service programs under the umbrella of one central organization and creating a new national service program: AmeriCorps.
—*National & Community—Government Support for Volunteering*[1]

Even if you think the items covered are elementary or obvious, in my experience it's important to make things clear so that everyone's on the same page from the outset. By doing so, you'll find that there will no gray areas. Everyone is given the same information and is specifically told what is expected of each person. For example, something as simple as maintaining confidentiality seems obvious, but I've found that this and the other issues listed must be not only mentioned but also clarified and emphasized to ensure compliance and consistency. For some volunteers, the rationale of a rule or policy is very important. Be sure to ask if the individual has questions as you go along. The handbook is also a convenient instrument to use for reviewing all your important training points.

"Training is useless unless you have a purpose; it's knowing for what purpose to train—for that can break men's fulfillment." This anonymous quote states plainly that training is important and necessary but needs to be purposeful. I agree. A clear purpose in your training plan will guide you in accomplishing your training goals. Spending time on preparation at the front end of your program will keep many problems from occurring and will provide a framework within which your volunteers and supervising staff can serve successfully.

To Recap

- Training will vary based upon the type and size of an organization.
- All training should include respect, responsibility, and accountability.
- A handbook can be a valuable tool.
- Having a plan will prevent numerous problems from occurring.

 STRUCTURING A VOLUNTEER PROGRAM

The loftier the building, the deeper must the foundation be laid.
—Thomas á Kempis

Without exception, structure is absolutely necessary if your program is going to be successful. Structure provides the foundation for growth and the underpinning for support once the program is up and running. In this chapter we focus on building a program from its inception and look at when to add leadership and what that involves as well as how it works. I'm going to use as an example an actual program that was started with five volunteers and grew to more than one hundred volunteers.

On Your Own

If you're the only staff member and have recruited one or two volunteers, you're the key leadership. Depending on your workload, one or two volunteers may be all the help you need. The number of volunteers needed will be determined after you complete the focus questions in chapter three and talk with staff.

Next Level

If you've identified multiple areas where volunteer staff members would be an asset and have been blessed with an influx of individuals who desire to serve, you're ready to move to the next level. In a sizeable organization, this level is reached when there are around twelve volunteers and is also determined by your stress level and the workload you can successfully manage. From the time you begin to add volunteers, be on the alert for individuals within this group who possess leadership skills. The team leader will come from this group. Here's what I've found is most important in a team leader:

- Well-liked by volunteers and staff members
- A good communicator
- Detail-orientated
- A servant's heart

Growing Pains

The mission organization I worked for was housed in a two-story building. The volunteer work area was on the first floor, and my office in the development department was on the second floor. As the number of volunteers grew, I quickly realized that I was going to have to make adjustments. Up until that point, each of our few volunteers worked alongside a staff member to whom he or she had been assigned.

It happened that at the same time the number of direct-mail letters we were mailing began to increase substantially. When the numbers were in the low hundreds, I printed them on a laser jet printer near my desk. It usually took one volunteer approximately an hour to stuff all the materials into envelopes. When a new development director was hired, the growth and resulting activity exploded.

Because of this change, the number of donors grew, increasing the number of direct-mail pieces. The new director also increased the frequency of direct mailings from quarterly to monthly. I quickly felt myself drowning in an increased workload and highly stressed. As the pressure intensified, it filtered down to the few volunteers who had been faithfully serving.

The number of our organization's field staff was growing as well, and each staff member had a monthly or quarterly newsletter he or she wanted to have mailed. This task was added to the volunteer workload.

First Block in the Structure

After a season of prayer, I went to the director and told him I needed help. Together we came up with a plan to increase the volunteer program. Not only did we need more volunteers, but I also wanted to turn some of my volunteer management duties over to other volunteers, since other regular staff members had heavy workloads too.

Because we had been paying attention to who was volunteering, the director and I knew which volunteer to approach about taking on more responsibilities. While we both committed the matter to prayer, we both agreed that Marti Petersen would be a good choice. She had been the go-to volunteer person for some time.

We called Marti and asked her to come in for an appointment with the two of us; the director had asked me put together a job description for her before the meeting. When she arrived, we opened the meeting with prayer, and the director presented the request. I explained the need and the job description. We asked Marti to pray about it and get back to us with her answer. We were both very thankful when she said yes, and our leadership structure began taking shape.

I typically worked through Marti, providing her with dates and numbers of upcoming direct-mail assignments. She then took responsibility for calling in the number of volunteers needed for the assignments. My responsibility was to have the needed materials ready and in place for the volunteers when they arrived.

We Need More Blocks

I asked the director and the CEO of the organization to talk to the volunteers about asking their friends, family members, and neighbors to come and volunteer. The director and the CEO also volunteered to visit the volunteers' Sunday School classes, home Bible study groups, senior groups, churches, and so on, to talk about the organization and our need for more volunteers.

It was also during this period that I asked to be included on the support staff meeting agenda and requested coworkers to present lists of volunteer tasks from their departments. I was asking for more work for the volunteers, but by this time the rest of the staff had seen the influx of new volunteers, and many began to understand their value firsthand. It was not long before they began asking for volunteer assistance. Growth was the byword of these years—at quantum levels.

As a result of the growth explosion, Marti was asked to extend her service term to two years, and we were thrilled when she agreed. She was excited and wanted to stay to see the program through a few growing pains. Through this experience grew our policy to request a two-year service commitment from the leadership volunteer. It wasn't until the second year of service that the leader was in full swing and could realize his or her full impact on the program.

A Couple, Please

Fairly early in this process we were all on the lookout for our next leader. Because of Marti's experience in the position and at her recommendation, we decided to look for a married couple who would serve together. We believed a couple could support each other and share the leadership tasks.

After a short period, one couple stood out—Lowell and Phyllis Andrews. The director, Leo, and Marti and I met with them and walked them through the first steps in the process, which had been updated because of the growth of the program. Lowell and Phyllis were not asked to take over immediately. We asked them to work alongside Marti as assistants/apprentices for two years, after which time we would evaluate the situation and make any necessary adjustments.

Marti graciously and effectively established the foundation for the program's structure. Lowell and Phyllis were able to take a well-established program and grow it from there. As a bonus, Marti stayed on as a volunteer, helping in the finance department and with direct mailings when extra help was needed.

As our volunteers gain skill and grow with Habitat, so does their capacity to take on greater leadership roles. The more leaders we grow, the more we can accomplish. Our increased organizational capacity is directly related to better managing and serving our volunteer base.

—*Anita Hellam, Habitat for Humanity*

A Well-Oiled Machine

As it turned out, Marti was right. A couple was an excellent solution for increasing and streamlining the program on many levels. Phyllis very ably handled the telephone scheduling. She also called to check on volunteers when they were sick or had other needs. She faithfully sent birthday and get-well cards to volunteers and provided get-well cards to be passed around for staff members to sign. Phyllis had the advantage of having worked as the receptionist at the organization for several years before retiring to volunteer, so she was well-known and liked by all the staff. She also greeted volunteers, welcomed new ones, took them on a tour of the facility, and introduced them to staff. Our goal was to help the volunteers know where things and people were, to feel comfortable, welcomed, wanted, and needed.

It was Lowell's responsibility to handle the instruction, explaining how to carry out the assigned tasks. After the tour with

Phyllis, Lowell would seat the new volunteer next to someone who had a good understanding of the direct-mail process and who could serve as an encourager. Every new person started out stuffing direct-mail letters, which also required matching names to envelopes. On the volunteer's first day, Lowell and Phyllis casually evaluated him or her and checked in frequently to assess his or her work. On especially busy days when Lowell or Phyllis couldn't check in with the new volunteer, they asked someone sitting close how the volunteer did.

These evaluations, along with the questionnaire and initial interview, gave leadership a fairly good idea of volunteers' skills and how the volunteers could most appropriately be utilized. Would they be suitable to help with specific staff members' requests, or did they need or prefer to stay with the direct-mail work? Some of Lowell's other responsibilities included introducing the morning speakers, leading in prayer, making announcements, and explaining the day's job. For a while Lowell and I met once a week to keep each other up-to-date and moving in the same direction.

Using an Assistant/Apprentice Couple

Leo and I advised Lowell and Phyllis from the outset to be on the lookout for another couple who could train alongside them as assistants/apprentices to eventually take over as the next lead couple.

God brought Marshall and Janet Jensen, a wonderful couple from Illinois. In fact, they moved to California just to do volunteer work. It was an unbelievable gift. Marshall and Janet had recently retired and were challenged during a visit from an old friend from California to come and serve. Thankfully, they stepped out to begin their faith journey.

During their time as assistants/apprentices, Marshall and Janet were given the opportunity to gain a clear understanding of how things worked, learn who was who, get to know the staff and allow the staff to get to know them, and learn what the mission was about.

The time for the switch of leadership to Marshall and Janet became apparent when Lowell injured his neck and back. Marshall and Janet had been well prepared and were able to step right in. Once Lowell got better, he and Phyllis continued to serve as volunteers and filled in when Marshall and Janet needed some time off.

As a result, Marshall, Janet, and I needed to be on the lookout for the next assistants/apprentices. Not surprisingly, we all agreed that Ken and Jan would be a good fit. The process began again as Ken and Jan were invited to a meeting.

How the Volunteer System Structure Works

Following is an overview of our non-profit organization's volunteer program structure, which took approximately four years to complete:

CEO
|
Department Director
|
Executive Assistant to Department Director
|
Assistant
|
Lead Volunteer Leadership Couple
|
Assistant/Apprentice Leadership Couple
|
Volunteers

Staff task requests were placed in an inbox and sent directly to the lead couple. The supply of extra request forms was available in a slot next to their inbox. When requests were received, the lead couple contacted the staff member to get additional information if it was needed and to let the staff member know when a skilled volunteer was available. The volunteer was scheduled to come in based on the staff member's request.

Establishing Communication Times Is Vital

I met formally with the volunteer leadership team at least twice a year. Our meetings included Laurie Freeman, the correspondence and task assistant. Laurie was of great assistance to me, handling many of the routine tasks and interactions with the volunteers. Her office was on the main floor next to the volunteer workroom.

Each year, as soon as the year-end mailing dates were set, I held one of the most important meetings of the year with the leadership team, usually during September. If the schedule allowed, I arranged to take everyone involved out to lunch and meet off campus. It was a special treat, because we all knew that the year-end activities meant an extremely heavy workload was just ahead. This normally included sending out hand-addressed Christmas cards, staff newsletters or Christmas cards, several direct-mail letters, the quarterly magazine, year-end giving records for tax purposes, plus making phone calls and sending CDs of public service announcements to United States radio stations.

At this meeting all members of the leadership team were given a list that included all project names, the dates of the mailings, number of pieces to be mailed, and the person responsible. After our meeting I also provided a larger twenty-by-twenty-four-inch copy of the list to be posted in the volunteer workroom so the volunteers would be aware of what was coming up as well.

At the monthly support staff meetings, I informed the staff of any changes, updates, and the year-end schedule. Staff members who needed to use volunteers during the year-end period had been asked to submit their request by a date in early September.

Laurie was available to the leadership team at all times. She was well-versed on postal regulations and stayed up-to-date on postage changes and ways to save money. She also served as a liaison between staff and the volunteer leadership team for times when minor problems arose or additional materials were required for a project to be completed.

If yours is an organization that sends multiple mailings, you may find that it will save your organization a great deal of money if there's someone on staff dedicated to knowing the ins and outs of postal service regulations and costs, as well as any rate changes that will affect your mailings. If you're the only person in the office, this will be another to-do item to add to your list. If you have a larger staff, talk with them and come to a decision about who will take on this responsibility. Mailings provide an important link to your constituents, and if you can search out ways to save money on mailings, that will be a big benefit to your organization.

Volunteer Communication Tool

Another form of communication came directly from the volunteer leadership team members themselves. Lowell says, "We felt strongly about writing a monthly newsletter directed to staff and volunteers—an open letter to staff asking them if they had any special needs with which volunteers could help. The newsletter might also contain prayer requests for persons on the volunteer team or staff or for family members. It could also keep staff informed about the volunteer workload and new additions to the volunteer team."

Must Be Accessible For Problem-Solving

As the organization grew, so did my responsibilities, and I was required to attend many meetings. I informed the leadership couples and Laurie that they could interrupt me if I was needed. I didn't want any projects ever to be put on hold because

I was in a meeting. We reached an understanding that if one of them stepped into the room where a meeting was being held, that was my cue that I was needed. Without a word, I would quietly get up and step out of the meeting or excuse myself from the conversation.

The team knew that my first question would be what steps they had taken to solve the problem. Early on, some of these "emergencies" turned into teaching times to help them learn to solve problems on their own. Nevertheless, I did not want them to hesitate to ask for my help. My goal was for them to know I was there to help and support them in any way I could.

Our program structure has ten steps, which begin with creating a profile of the volunteer needed and ending with the evaluation and long-term relationship of the volunteer. We have a manager for each department and two volunteer coordinators, one per office. Each volunteer has a tutor-manager and a coordinator in a more institutional role.
—*Carolina Villanueva, Manager, Intern and Volunteer Department, Idealistas.org, Buenos Aires*

The Working of the Team—Added Benefits

Having two couples, one in an assistant-apprentice role, proved to be very beneficial to the two couples, the volunteer staff, and me. As the organization grew, we came to the point at which we needed to utilize volunteers two days a week rather than one. It worked well for one leadership couple to be responsible for one day's work and the other couple to take responsibility for the second day. Also, since the leadership teams were retired and enjoyed traveling, they would be able to fill in for each other. During especially busy times, such as year-end mailings, both couples worked both days, and they switched off leading the team one day and performing in a supporting role the other.

Goal

Structure is the foundation of a successful volunteer program. The goal is to establish a system that allows for growth as your volunteer numbers increase and to provide support for those in leadership positions. The need is to keep your leadership team encouraged and informed and to prevent burnout. Having an assistant-apprentice couple is a constructive step in that direction and has the added benefit of providing on-the-job training. It also allows for a smooth transition from one head leadership couple to another. Even if you choose not to use couples, I highly recommend having an assistant-apprentice structure in place once your program has grown beyond your ability to oversee it yourself.

2002: President George W. Bush created USA Freedom Corps, a White House office to coordinate national volunteer efforts in response to the terrorist attacks of September 11, 2001. Beyond the existing AmeriCorps, Senior Corps, Peace Corps, and Learn and Serve America programs, USA Freedom Corps spurs the creation of several new volunteer programs aimed specifically at securing the nation, including Citizen Corps Councils in the United States and territories. In addition, the president calls on all Americans to devote the equivalent of two years of their lives—4,000 hours—to service and volunteering.

—National & Community Service
Government Support for Volunteering[1]

To Recap

- One volunteer is a beginning.
- A couple is extremely beneficial in carrying out all the necessary leadership responsibilities.
- As quickly as you locate the first leadership couple, start looking for an apprentice-assistant couple.

- Communicate, communicate, communicate. Establish strong lines of communication between you and the volunteer leadership team, the leadership team and the volunteers, and you and the support staff.

HANDLING PROBLEMS

Problems are only opportunities in work clothes.
—Henry J. Kaiser

In addition to their many valuable skills and personal qualities, volunteers are also individuals with needs, hurts, and troubles. Each person brings an opportunity for caring by you and the staff, as well as an ideal way to demonstrate your organization's mission statement.

Looking for the Door

Jack (not his real name) was not too happy to be there. His wife had been volunteering for several months and enjoyed her time with the other volunteers, and she strongly encouraged Jack to join her. But Jack didn't see anything going on in the office that was interesting to him. In fact, he was looking for the door when I encountered him.

I asked him if he would like to be a regular volunteer. His immediate response was an unequivocal no. He then tempered his reply with the explanation that he and his wife loved to travel in their recreational vehicle and couldn't commit to a regular schedule.

I assured him we had activities for people who could help only occasionally and asked him what interested him. Again, he was explicit in saying he had no interests connected with office work. In fact, the idea of doing repetitive work of any kind was distasteful to him.

Wondering just what would inspire him to even think about volunteer work, I asked him what he liked to do. He said he enjoyed being outside in the fresh air, getting dirt under his fingernails. I couldn't turn the gardening over to him, since we needed regular lawn and garden care and couldn't arrange it around his sporadic schedule.

Feeling the defeat of the moment, I sent up a quick prayer for inspiration. What about changing the flowers in the flowerbeds each spring and fall? Our gardeners currently offered this service at an extra cost. I thought Jack could take on this task, maintaining a flexible time schedule, and it would give him the opportunity to be outside in the fresh air and dig in the dirt.

When I mentioned planting flowers to Jack, he brightened and began to ask questions about when it needed to be done and what kind of flowers we wanted to have planted. We put together a schedule for him, and he began to plan for the spring planting, which would be coming up in just a few weeks. We would pay for the flowers, and he would provide the labor.

It turned out that Jack was a master gardener, one who knew the right way to plant flowers and how to prevent diseases in the flowerbeds. When he arrived on the agreed-to day, his truck was full of tools and many containers of seasonal flowers. He enriched the soil and meticulously planted the flowers in neat rows. Jack was clearly in his element, and he beamed each time someone came by to compliment him on the work.

The flowerbeds surrounding our mission building never looked better. The plants flourished under Jack's care, and each fall and spring a new batch was planted to beautify the property. Jack loved to hear from me when I thought it was time to replant. He would soon arrive, his truck bed bulging with flowers, planting soil, and tools.

Jack eventually began to stretch his volunteering to other areas. Soon he was a regular, volunteering to stuff envelopes, do light maintenance work, and be useful in many ways. He and his wife continued to travel and take care of family needs, but whenever they were in town, he was around to get plugged in wherever he could help. This reluctant volunteer became a valuable member of the team, but it took some creative thinking to get him to that place (*Larry Koch, retired facilities manager for a nonprofit organization*).

They're Talking Instead of Working

Volunteers don't work with your organization only to perform your list of tasks. For many, the act of volunteering provides a wonderful opportunity for fellowship. Some volunteers may not have much interaction with others, and volunteering might be their main outing for the week. However, there needs to be a middle ground. The goal is to find a balance between visiting and working.

When volunteers are working in a large group, there will be lots of socializing. This is to be expected, but the volunteers occasionally need to be encouraged to keep moving along with the work assignment. I leave this to the volunteer leadership team to determine and oversee. They know the work that needs to be completed on any given day and have the skill to help people focus, often in a humorous way that keeps everyone happy.

Here's what to do if you are assigned a volunteer who only wants to talk. Again, try to find a balance. It's important to develop relationships, but the work must also get done. The solution could be as simple as a gentle reminder at the appropriate moment or a less confrontational group reminder when the entire volunteer group is together. Seating assignments can also be arranged to split up the talkers if necessary. Don't let the situation build. Deal with it when it happens, using humor or a firm but gracious comment. Don't wait. It will only get worse.

We have zero tolerance for certain things. There can be no drug or alcohol consumption or residual effects of such use while people are working at Habitat. We have and we do dismiss people immediately for being inebriated. This does not apply only to illegal drugs; if prescription drugs cause similar symptoms, the person cannot work. If the problem is simply cultural—for example, foul or abusive language—a discreet word from the supervisor expressing the expectations usually changes the behavior. If a problem volunteer is not willing to follow our rules, he or she is asked to leave.

—Anita Hellam, Habitat for Humanity

Material Problems

The shortage of needed materials was a problem that came up frequently at the organization where I worked. This is a problem that must be addressed at the staff level. If a staff member is consistently late or short of materials, set up a meeting with him or her to get the problem on the table, and work together to find a solution.

After running short of printed materials on several occasions, the print clerk and I explored the mystery of running out of copies when the counter on the printer showed we had the correct number. We had a cantankerous folding machine that was known to eat copies. We accommodated the folding machine by running a specific number of extras with each print job. But sometimes we were still short. Upon further investigation, we discovered other staff members were often unaware when we were printing a big job and would send their own print jobs to the printer, interrupting our job and escalating the number on the counter.

We remedied this problem by placing a sign on the printer several hours in advance, letting others know when we would run our project and how long it would take. In addition, it was decided as a team always to run a set number of extra copies. This strategy worked well most of the time.

We also had a problem with the materials not being in the volunteer workroom and ready for the volunteers to start work when they arrived. This dilemma was solved in discussion at a support staff meeting. We agreed all materials must be on the volunteer work table the morning *before* the job was to be completed.

At the organization where I worked, one volunteer would come in the day before the main group of volunteers was expected to fold any materials via a folding machine. If you don't have a folding machine, then this particular task will need to be incorporated into the other volunteer group tasks. If the materials were not in place, the job would be postponed until the following week. It took delaying only one job for the guilty staff member to get on board.

When dealing with such situations, state specifically what the consequences will be, and then follow through when a lapse occurs. It's human nature that when people get away with something, whether through carelessness or poor planning, they'll continue to operate in the same sloppy manner unless there are specific consequences. These lapses waste valuable time and are disrespectful of the volunteers.

Volunteer Complaints About Staff or Other Volunteers

The solution to dealing with complaints about staff or other volunteers is simple. Don't get in the middle of the situation. Tell the volunteer to speak to a volunteer leadership team member. Getting in the middle will cause problems for you with both the staff member and the volunteer leadership. Your goal is to remain neutral and focused.

Postage Machine Upkeep

Assign the task of checking the postage machine to a specific individual to be done a few days before each large mailing. Allow plenty of time to replenish the postage if needed. The assignment can be included on the leadership team's checklist in preparation for a volunteer work day, or a staff member can be designated to check the machine weekly as part of his or her job description.

This cannot be left to chance. Postage machines that are not regularly maintained have a way of running out of postage right in the middle of an important mailing deadline.

Equipment Problems

A general policy should be established that only a trained and approved volunteer will be assigned or allowed to use machines or equipment. Proper training helps prevent unnecessary equipment failures, injuries, and loss of valuable production time.

A volunteer advisory committee (leadership team) is the appropriate body to review issues and problems. These issues are discussed with the staff person or director, and the director makes the final decision.

—Leo H. Cullum

Preventing Costly Mistakes

We once had a volunteer who jumped ahead and ran a mailing before checking to see what amount of postage each piece required. While the volunteer's initiative was appreciated, she was unaware that there are money-saving ways to sort and bundle mailings. We prevented a recurrence of this mistake by assigning only staff-trained volunteers to oversee this task—no exceptions. We made sure there was a minimum of two volunteers trained for this assignment so they could work together and share the workload.

If there are no trained volunteers available, then the task should be handled only by a staff member. Again, using the correct postage can save your organization a substantial amount of money.

When Volunteers Refuse Staff Members' Requests

Stress seemed to be a constant companion when I worked at an international nonprofit organization with thousands of direct-mail pieces, staff newsletters, a quarterly magazine, and other mailing materials to be processed by volunteers regularly. Tension sometimes ran high among both volunteers and staff. Once, in the middle of a stressful project, a staff member reported to me that a volunteer had refused to perform a task that she had requested.

The staff member told the volunteer, Sam (not his real name), that a newsletter mailing had to be done a specific way as requested by field staff. Sam refused. From my point of view, the matter was made worse by the fact that Sam was a member of the volunteer leadership team. I worked directly with the volunteer leadership team, and they in turn ran the volunteer program. I had trained them to always say yes to the staff person assigning the job, and then together we would figure out any resulting challenges. This was not the first time this individual had exhibited defiant behavior, and I knew a confrontation was inevitable.

At the heart of this issue was Sam's attitude. The attitude I sought to foster among staff toward volunteers was gratitude and respect, that of a servant.

I had previously spoken with Sam regarding his attitude, as had our mailroom expert who worked with the volunteers every day. We usually handled problems such as this in the following way:

- We asked the volunteer to step away from the working volunteer group to a private place before addressing the problem with the volunteer.
- We spoke to both the staff member and the volunteer, sometimes bringing them together, and listened to what each had to say, asking questions to make sure we had a clear picture of what had taken place.
- We attempted to reinforce the servanthood concept and how those principles could be applied in each situation by the volunteer. We encouraged the staff member to be openly respectful and grateful toward the volunteer.

Both Laurie and I had walked through these steps with Sam on several occasions. Each time I had been a bit stronger in my presentation. For Sam to refuse the staff member's request and walk away was a tipping point for me, and it signaled a situation in need of immediate intervention.

I thanked the staff member for coming to me and told her I would take care of it. Then I walked downstairs, praying the entire way. I approached Sam and quietly asked if I could speak with him. We walked out of the workroom and into an empty office, where I asked him if he had told the staff member no. In a clipped tone of voice, he said, "Yes, I did—and I would again." At this point, Sam was ready to leave and rejoin the main group.

Having anticipated his reaction, I was already standing directly in his path, and in a soft but firm voice, looking him directly in the eyes, I slowly told him, "You will never tell a staff member no again. Do you understand me?" I finally had his attention. I said it again, not unkindly but tolerating no argument and added, "I'm here to help you if you have a problem. I know this is an extremely busy time, but you will never tell a staff member no again. Do you understand?"

He didn't say anything, so I continued. "You're a volunteer. You can choose to be here or not, but if you are here you will never tell a staff member no again. Do you understand?" He visibly softened, stopping long enough to internalize the impact of my words.

"Yes," he said. "I'm sorry."

I told him I wasn't the person who needed the apology. Thankfully, he apologized to the staff member, and we never had another issue like that again.

It's important to use these events as teaching opportunities, assuring the offender that you're in this with him or her for the long-haul. My aim was always to evaluate and understand the situation from two perspectives: the growth of the volunteer, and the task requested by the staff member.

When a Staff Member and Volunteer Are Married

In my experience, a spouse volunteering in the same area where his or her spouse works is not a good situation for several reasons. It has the potential of putting other staff members on the spot. This is especially true if the volunteering spouse inadvertently creates more work, is performing a task incorrectly, or just wants to hang around his or her spouse. Having the volunteer in the department can also cause the employee to hover over the spouse, or the volunteering spouse may expect special treatment.

Even more problematic is that sometimes the volunteer will look to the spouse to call the shots instead of deferring to the volunteer leadership team. If the spouse of an employee expresses a desire to volunteer, he or she should go through the questionnaire process just like everyone else. It may be that the spouse would prefer to volunteer in a different area but the staff member is pushing the spouse to volunteer in his or her department. Establish as early as possible that staff spouses are welcome and encouraged to volunteer, but not in an area where the employed spouse is working or is responsible.

One staff member shared the following story:

From time to time Martha (not her real name) would come to the office to help out. Her job was to file documents, but she never became familiar with the filing system. As a result, she had frequent questions for the two support staff members in the department, constantly interrupting their work. To complicate things, Martha was the wife of the department head. Whenever she was there, he was constantly hovering. Don't get me wrong—Martha is delightful. However, a different assignment would have been appropriate, such as helping with the monthly mailings, where she and the other volunteers could socialize to their hearts' content as they worked.

The problem we encountered by allowing Martha to work in her husband's department was that it created confusion about who should be calling the shots relative to her work assignment. This dilemma had the effect of unsettling everyone concerned, including Martha, the volunteer supervisor, and the two employees in the department.

To deal with problems that might arise, we usually have regular meetings with the volunteers and talk everything through. The tutor is responsible for detecting problems and the coordinator for helping find solutions. The evaluation always helps to improve past flaws.

—*Carolina Villanueva, Manager of Intern and Volunteer Department, Idealistas.org, Buenos Aires*

Volunteers Who Insist On Doing Things "My Way"

There should always be a predetermined standard for every volunteer task, but sometimes there may be different ways to arrive at that standard. As a case in point, when stuffing items into an envelope for direct mailings, people who are left-handed need to set up the materials in a different order than right-handed people. This shouldn't be a problem as long as all the pieces are in the correct place inside the envelope once completed.

On occasion, you may have a strong-willed and stubborn individual on your hands who insists on doing things his or her own way. In this event, clearly state that this is the way the boss wants it. Don't let yourself get upset. Take a deep breath, and graciously show the person again how the job should be done. You might take the soft approach by saying, "I probably didn't communicate what we needed very well." If after the demonstration there are still issues with the volunteer's performance of the task, inform the leadership team member, and suggest that the volunteer be reassigned to someone else or to other tasks.

Here's how this issue was handled in a group setting by the volunteer leadership team members:

- Show volunteers how the finished product will look.
- Demonstrate how the task should be done.
- If the way demonstrated doesn't work for a particular volunteer, give him or her the freedom to do it a different way, as long as the finished product looks like the one that was demonstrated.

According to one volunteer leadership team member, "It's important to recognize that everyone works differently; it's okay to let people do things their way as long as quality is maintained. When the volunteer doesn't want to complete the task to the standard that has been set by the person requesting the help, I would ask, 'If you had the choice, how would you do it?' After walking through this process, the individual will normally see that a lot of time and experience has gone into completing the task to a specific level of quality. I've found that when each task given is explained and demonstrated, allowing the volunteer to repeat what was shown, problems are usually eliminated."

Older Volunteer Won't Take Instructions from Younger Staff Member

The situation of an older volunteer who won't take instructions from a younger staff member can be touchy, and you probably won't even know it's a problem until after it happens. In other words, it's not something you can generally anticipate. Here's an example of how this might occur.

The staff member requested a volunteer to help complete a task that would take several weeks. The volunteer was called and a date set for her to come in. The volunteer met with the staff member, who explained and demonstrated the job. The volunteer started the job, but when she had questions, she wouldn't ask the staff member. Instead, she kept working, and her frustration built. After the volunteer left for the day, the staff member checked her work, and there were problems.

The next week when the volunteer arrived to work, the staff member demonstrated what she needed again and asked if the volunteer had any questions, encouraging her to ask. The volunteer didn't admit to having any problems and asked no questions. This time when the volunteer did the work, she was more frustrated, and she started to get angry. No one was aware this was going on until the volunteer went to the staff member's supervisor and blew up.

The staff member had no idea that the volunteer was so upset. Once the supervisor started asking questions, it was discovered the volunteer didn't feel that she should have to ask questions from anyone younger than herself, and she refused to take directions from a "kid." She would do the work her own way.

After listening calmly, the supervisor told the volunteer, "That's the way I asked for the task to be completed. The staff member is only carrying out my request, doing it the way I asked her to do it."

The volunteer was speechless. The supervisor then said, "It's obvious this situation isn't working for you. Let's see if we can get you reassigned to another task." Unfortunately, this particular volunteer continued to have problems even after she was reassigned—and was not called to come back. Attitude is key, and it's your choice as to who you have serving at your organization.

You certainly don't want an ongoing situation that creates more problems than it solves.

Staff Interruptions

What if you have a talkative staff member who likes to spend time chatting with volunteers? A group of volunteers is all the more enticing, because now the employee has a ready-made audience. The first step in addressing this problem is to speak privately with the staff member, right after one of his or her "appearances." This discussion is often all that's needed.

If the staff member continues to take an extensive amount of volunteer time socializing, speak to him or her again, making it clear that if it continues, you'll have a talk with his or her boss. Then follow through if it happens again.

Bear in mind, however, that there isn't anything inherently wrong with staff members stopping by. In fact, staff members should be encouraged to stop by and greet and thank the volunteers for their service. The kind of interruptions I'm talking about are long periods that distract the volunteers' attention from their assignments. This kind of behavior is counterproductive to the volunteers' work and their time spent with your organization. Establishing a few guidelines for staff ahead of time will go a long way toward preventing lengthy interruptions.

Too Few or Too Many Volunteers

Having too few volunteers requires your focus to be on recruiting. See chapter three for ideas.

Believe it or not, having too little work for volunteers sometimes happens. Each time it occurred, I requested a few minutes during a support staff meeting to present the problem, asking for more jobs for the volunteers. Invariably, additional requests were submitted for volunteer assistance. You could also send out and receive this same information via e-mail if it's more convenient.

They Work Too Slowly

Volunteers will work at different speeds. When an individual seemed to lag behind in a certain task, I tried to assign that person to work on something not involving a time crunch. In cases where the slower individual was working in a group doing something such as a direct mailing, the volunteer leadership knew to give that person a smaller number of envelopes to complete during the same period. In this way, the volunteer experienced success and was able to enjoy the fellowship with the other volunteers while helping the entire group finish the assignment.

To Recap

- Occasionally a relationship problem may occur, but hopefully within Christian circles there will be fewer problems. When problems do occur, you'll likely find that there have been misunderstandings as to how the given task or situation was interpreted by the volunteer.
- Problems usually show up quickly and need to be handled promptly, calmly, directly, and lovingly.
- Each volunteer brings an opportunity to demonstrate Christ's love.

KEEPING VOLUNTEERS HAPPY

Volunteers are not paid not because they are worthless but because they are priceless.
—Anonymous

In 1974 United States President Richard Nixon signed an executive order to establish National Volunteer Week as an annual celebration of volunteering. Every year since, each president, along with many governors, mayors, and other elected officials, has signed a proclamation setting aside a specific week to acknowledge the value of volunteers to the country.

This week could serve as an excellent starting point for the recognition of your own volunteers. The National Service Resources Web site is a great place to begin. It provides the dates of the recognition week for the next few years. The address for the Web site is <http://nationalserviceresources.org/node/20302>.

Another extremely useful Web site related to this topic is Positive Promotions, at <www.postivepromotions.com>. This site will provide you with suggested themes for this special week and items you can purchase related to that theme. You can call their experienced customer service department directly at 1-800-635-2666, or order online at <www.positivepromotions.com>.

I discovered that finding ways to thank and recognize the volunteers was one of the best parts of my job. Of course, we participated in National Volunteer Week, but I actively looked for additional opportunities to recognize volunteers in as many ways as possible throughout the entire year. I also encouraged staff members with an assigned volunteer to come up with their own methods of personally thanking and encouraging their volunteer. The need for recognition is very important to most people, and a common complaint by volunteers is that they don't feel needed or appreciated by the staff. Give your volunteer frequent and sincere recognition and appreciation through a variety of methods.

Following are some ideas we have used to recognize volunteers. Some worked well, and some did not. We'll examine these ideas and share comments we received from some of the volunteers.

National Volunteer Week

I would love to say that I always planned a year in advance for National Volunteer Week, but that wouldn't be the truth. I was usually reminded of it when I received the promotional catalog from Positive Promotions (<www.postivepromotions.com>, 800-635-2666). The catalog has materials available for organizations to purchase that are based on the current year's theme and also includes other items from past years. One nice feature of the catalog is a stapled insert that contains numerous suggestions on ways to show appreciation to your volunteers. I found this to be an excellent resource.

Because we scheduled another time of the year to conduct an all-out appreciation event, National Volunteer Week was low-keyed. One year we purchased a banner that proclaimed, "We Love Our Volunteers!" We kept that banner in the volunteer workroom for years. Most years I purchased colorful balloons and asked the staff to wear labeled badges that proudly declared, "I love my volunteers." About two weeks in advance,

I sent an e-mail letting the staff know the dates and theme for that year's National Volunteer Week. The message also included an encouragement to the staff to go out of their way to personally thank as many volunteers as possible throughout the week. A week prior to National Volunteer Week, I placed a note with two sticker badges in each staff member's mailbox. These were to be worn during the two days when the majority of the volunteers were in the office. I also sent out another e-mail to the staff on the Monday of Volunteer Week, reminding them that it was National Volunteer Week and encouraging them to wear their badges. Our weekly all-staff meeting gave me the opportunity to again encourage everyone to express appreciation personally to as many volunteers as possible throughout the week.

During National Volunteer Week the colorful balloons suspended in the reception area, volunteer workroom, and break area created a festive atmosphere in the office.

I never feel that I adequately thank everyone who supports us. So many deeds are unseen or unrecognized. We do have an annual appreciation dinner, and we invite key volunteers to be recognized. For those who fall under the radar, I hope they're filled with personal satisfaction knowing that they have made a difference.

—*Anita Hellam, Habitat for Humanity*

President's Volunteer Service Awards

You can become a "certifying organization" and nominate qualifying volunteers for the President's Volunteer Service Award at <www.presidentialserviceawards.gov>. This site offers the possibility of nationally recognizing your volunteers for their dedication and support. It also provides a wonderful story for your local paper or news outlet. It's positive information your local news sources are looking for and will also afford a promotional opportunity for your organization. Remember to ask the news source to include your contact information in the article or at the end of it.

Valentine's Day

Whenever I've been in charge of a volunteer program, I've set aside Valentine's Day for special focus of celebration. There are two reasons. First, Valentine's Day is an established day in our culture for showing and expressing love. Second, the majority of the volunteers I've worked with in churches and nonprofit organizations are retired. The largest percent of these individuals are single women who are alone for different reasons, but mostly because they are widows. Because they are usually not honored on Valentine's Day, this event gives them a reason to get dressed up and be treated like royalty.

This event was "certainly worth the time," states Paul Calhoun, former CEO of a central California nonprofit. "It served to motivate volunteers and give them a sense of how deeply they were appreciated. Our communication to them underlined the great things God was doing through our organization. This helped to establish their impact of being an integral part of something worldwide, something of eternal significance."

This is how we used to celebrate the event:

- Each year I created a special invitation that incorporated the Valentine's Day theme.
- Invitations were mailed one month in advance of the event. It became such an anticipated affair that volunteers put it on their calendars a year ahead of time. The date was always the closest working day to February 14.
- The organization sponsored a wonderful brunch at an off-site location. As a rule, brunch is less expensive than lunches or dinners—to a certain extent because of the food selection but also because the venues seem to have more time and space available during that time slot. I always made a

point of finding a restaurant that would give us a great price for our event. Don't just take someone else's opinion; get out there and do the research. Ask if the venue offers discounts to nonprofits. You'll be glad you did, and your organization will be blessed because you've saved it money.

- On the day of the event, staff members arrived early to greet volunteers as they entered the room. The staff also hosted tables and served the coffee, tea, and so on. To personalize the event, only staff members who had used volunteers during the previous year were invited to attend. This policy was not meant to exclude or punish anyone, but it frequently served as a motivation for staff who had been reluctant to use volunteer helpers. Case in point: Sharon (not her real name), a staff member, told me in no uncertain terms, "I don't need volunteers." My internal response to that statement was *You don't have a clue*, but externally I said, "Of course, that's your choice." Then Valentine's Day rolled around, and nearly the entire office was gone for the whole morning having a great time. The holdouts were left behind. As people returned to the office, there was lots of laughter and goodwill returning with them. The whole atmosphere of the office was upbeat and festive. When I got back to the workplace later, Sharon, as I expected, immediately came up to my office and wanted to talk. "Why didn't I get invited to the Valentine's Day brunch?" she asked. I said, "Well, did you use a volunteer last year?" Her face dropped. I continued: "The brunch is to show appreciation to the volunteers." Enough said. Within the next few days Sharon discovered ways a volunteer could help her. She attended the brunches from then on.
- A nametag station manned by two staff members was situated at the entry door to the banquet room.
- A staff member took each volunteer's photo and other candid shots throughout the morning.

- Staff members were encouraged to fill their tables with volunteers. If a staff member worked with a specific volunteer, a seat was saved for him or her at the table the staff member hosted.

- Because Valentine's Day is not too long after the State of the Union speech by the President of the United States, I initiated what we called the "State of the Mission" address, which the CEO gave every year at this event. It was a chance for the CEO to talk about all the great things the mission had accomplished the year before with the volunteers' help. He also addressed some of the new and exciting things that would be happening in the year ahead. The volunteers were often the first to be entrusted with this new information about the future of our organization, giving them a feeling of being trusted and honored.

- When a new video was created to promote the mission, we arranged to "premier" it at the volunteer brunch.

- The Valentine's Day event was also an occasion to give a gift to each volunteer. Although I've already talked about this in a previous chapter, I feel the point is important enough to repeat. Every gift you give must have your organization's logo, name, and some form of contact information on it, if at all possible. The volunteers serve as your ambassadors to the world. Make the gift something that will spark a conversation and give them the opportunity to talk about your wonderful organization. In the process of purchasing the gift each year, I always bought extras for the staff, board, special vendors, and donors. The staff received their gifts after the volunteers had been given theirs. It invariably became a poorly kept secret what the yearly gift was going to be. Although we tried to keep it hush-hush, it was the staff who always pressed to find out early each year.

- For event centerpieces I often used a medium-size potted plant with a colorful foil wrapper that matched our theme colors. I also secretly placed some type of marker at one chair at each table, making sure not to select a chair occupied by a staff member. The person sitting at the place with the marker would then be revealed at the end of the event and be given the plant to take home. Some years I used other methods to determine the selection, such as giving the centerpiece to the person at the table whose birthday was the closest to the 14th.

I highly recommend using Valentine's Day as the focus for a yearly appreciation event for your volunteers. The benefits and rewards are many.

To express appreciation to our volunteers, we have a benefit program for them that includes free snacks and lunches, training sessions, certificates, and goodbye gifts. Also we have an agreement with a public university this year for discounts in nonprofit careers. We host gatherings with them and constantly thank them for their hard work.
—*Carolina VIllanueva, Manager, Intern and Volunteer Department, Idealistas.org, Buenos Aires*

Weekly Ways to Show Appreciation

You'll request most volunteers to work at your organization on a weekly basis. Acknowledge them and their service in some way every time they come in to volunteer. Never take them for granted. They're a gift, not a given. The most effective recognition occurs in the day-to-day dealings between staff and volunteers. Staff expressions of appreciation and thanks for ongoing work are extremely powerful types of recognition. Following are a few ideas we developed to establish an atmosphere of appreciation for our volunteers. Some of these ideas came directly from the volunteers and some from staff members.

- A coffee break was provided, whether the volunteers were working in a large group or individually. The individuals were encouraged by their respective staff member or a volunteer leadership team member to participate in the coffee break time. Along with coffee, donuts were offered.
- During the break time, a staff member often spoke to the group about the role staff members filled at the mission. Frequently the speaker was a field staff member, showing slides or sharing photos and telling about their latest trip overseas. Many times the volunteers were able to view photos before anyone else on staff got a chance to see them. On other occasions, a headquarters' staff member might talk about how his or her role contributed to the overall mission. There was always a question-and-answer period afterward, and the volunteers looked forward to these sessions. They knew they were hearing "insider information." The speaker gave the volunteers the opportunity to learn firsthand about the people throughout the world whose lives were being impacted by the work of the mission. Here is a comment from a field staff member who spoke during these times, whose name is withheld for security reasons: "I enjoyed every opportunity I was provided to talk to the volunteers. It was great to be able to meet and get to know them and tell them about the field work. They had great questions and seemed genuinely interested in the work. I know they prayed for me, too. They were such an encouragement to me personally."
- Unique to our organization was the fact that our CEO took no salary and volunteered in his position. He did a wonderful job of aligning himself with the volunteers. His executive assistant and I worked to schedule him to speak to the volunteers on the days when the most volunteers were in the building. The volunteers loved him, and he loved and genuinely appreciated them. This encouraged

goodwill and added value to the volunteers. They knew they were important and that the CEO cared about them. The CEO remembers: "They frequently let me know how much they appreciated and prayed for our team. Their enthusiasm inevitably encouraged me." The point is to get your leadership involved. It helps them understand what's going on and adds significance to the volunteers' work. It's a win-win situation for everyone.

- The wife of our head leadership team sent birthday, anniversary, and get-well cards to volunteers. When longer illnesses or hospitalizations occurred, a card was made available for the staff to sign as well.
- Leadership team members occasionally telephoned the volunteers just to talk with and stay connected with them.

Increase Your Appreciation Atmosphere.

The atmosphere you create for your volunteers is a snowball that gains momentum as it rolls along. At first it will feel as if it's all about you and your efforts. You may even feel as if nothing is happening, but hang in there. Keep working at it and praying. Before you know it, people will believe the great atmosphere has always been there. The following points may seem very simple but can be vital to developing an atmosphere in which volunteers are happy and eager to return:

- Maintain a bulletin board in the main volunteer work area. When I first put up a bulletin board, I posted some of the candid photos taken at the Valentine's Day event. We also had all the photos out on the work tables that day for the volunteers to see. If any of them wanted a copy of one of the photos, we provided it. The volunteer leadership team assumed the task of maintaining the bulletin board, but I occasionally put something on it such as a photo, a special thank-you note from a donor, a meaningful quotation, or a word of encouragement.

- I placed a postcard with a pretty border in each staff member's in-box with a note asking him or her to write a word of encouragement to the volunteers in general—not to a specific volunteer. The staff members were requested to place the notes in my in-box and I posted them around the volunteer workroom for the volunteers to read.
- A few times a year I put out a pretty bowl containing a candy treat of some kind. Once I came across mints wrapped in paper imprinted with a special thank-you message specifically for volunteers at <www.PositivePromotions.com>.
- Be flexible. Volunteers are not employees. True, some volunteers become so valuable and dependable that you may tend to forget that they're volunteers. But they should never be pressured to come in. This is a service, not an obligation. They should be treated as special guests in a home.
- Protect volunteers from others coming to them and giving them work or telling them what to do. There needs to be one leadership team, and leadership is in charge. It was important to me to reinforce the volunteer leadership team's role, so I told them things I wanted the volunteers to know. The information needed to come through the leadership team since they were in charge of the volunteers.
- There are reasons volunteers keep coming back that have nothing to do with anything the organization does except provide the opportunity of service. Along with that opportunity, the volunteers themselves develop a warm, friendly, and inviting working atmosphere. In my own experience, this is in many ways the most powerful reason volunteers return again and again. Consider the following examples of actual anonymous comments made by volunteers when asked why they returned:
  - I developed friendships.
  - People showed an interest in each other.
  - I had fun, and we laughed together.

- We prayed for each other and became aware of needs.
- We encouraged one another, not only during our time in the office but also away from the office.
- We truly became a family during our times together.
- When I knew there was a demanding volunteer job that was going to be especially stressful and time-consuming for a large number of volunteers, I planned something extra. For example, if the task was going to take them past the lunch hour, I ordered pizzas for the group. This usually occurred during the nonprofit organization's year-end mailing push. There were multiple mailings squeezed into a short span of time, and a large number of volunteers were coming in for several days a week. When situations such as this occur, it's a good time to show your appreciation. Another choice might be to have pies brought in for them to enjoy at break time.
- Create a laminated thank-you bookmark with one or more photos of someone who has been touched by your organization. It could also contain a word of thanks from the staff, CEO, or board, or an encouraging verse or quotation.
- Put together a volunteer thank-you kit in a party goodie bag—including items such as candies, cookies, fudge, a votive candle, and special tea bags. Be creative. You could include a number and variety of items at very little cost to the organization by shopping at a local dollar store, purchasing things found in a closeout bin, or buying in bulk at a discount outlet. Include a thank-you note or a small thank-you gift tag.
- Photo scrapbook: Find a person on staff who just loves to scrapbook. Provide him or her with all the candid snapshots and event photos that have been taken over a given year. Encourage the staff person to be creative. This scrapbook should be displayed in an area where volunteers and staff can view it at will. If creativity isn't your strong suit,

be sure to find someone to place the photos in a photo album. This could be an ongoing volunteer task, and the photos can be added throughout the years. If someone is willing to take this on as a project, reimburse him or her for a reasonable amount of supplies to enhance the project. The completed project will serve as a remembrance and encouragement for staff and volunteers.

Service to others is the payment you make for your space here on earth.
—*Muhammad Ali*

It has been mentioned before, but it's so important that your staff, from the CEO on down, makes it a practice to express appreciation to the volunteers in as many ways as possible. It takes only a moment to thank a volunteer when you see him or her carrying out a task or walking around your organization. Nametags will facilitate this act of kindness, alerting the staff members by identifying who the volunteers are. Remind the staff during staff meetings, via e-mail, and individually to take a moment of their time to thank volunteers. By all means, however, keep it genuine. The expressions should always be sincere.

I would occasionally pop into the CEO's office and mention when there were volunteers in the building. When the head of the organization mingles with the volunteers, it's very meaningful to them. Your expressions of thanks don't need to be a formal proclamation. Just stop by the area occasionally when volunteers are working and say, "Thank you." This doesn't need to be a speech to the whole group. Keep it simple and authentic.

Prayer

Faith-based organizations have an enormous advantage over other kinds of nonprofits. I believe prayer is the single most important factor in having a successful volunteer program. I've chosen to mention it in this chapter because I feel it's also essential in keeping volunteers happy and eager to return. Simply put, your prayers for each volunteer and his or her work, each leadership team member, and the staff when they're sick, hurting, or rejoicing are vitally important. Pray consistently for your volunteers. If you have volunteers assigned to specific staff members, that staff member should pray for his or her personal volunteer, solicit the prayers of others, and even take time to pray with the volunteer personally.

While prayer has been a central feature of my personal walk with the Lord, that's not the reason it took such a place of honor and contributed to such a high degree to the success of the volunteer program. The fact is, our CEO, Paul Calhoun, had a motto that was central to the success of the mission organization: "No prayer, no results." It was the fundamental theme and focus of his own life, and he inspired the mission to adopt it as a practical, indispensable daily component of the ministry.

Prayer permeated every corner and undergirded every action of the organization. Weekly staff gatherings over lunch ended in an extended time of prayer. Staff members paired up in rotating groups to meet once a week for fifteen minutes to pray for each other and the concerns of the mission. A few staff members also chose to meet daily in small groups for prayer before the day's business began.

Once a year the organization participated in a "Worldwide Day of Prayer," which included the international staff praying in their respective countries. Throughout the year there were calls to halt work and pray for special needs that occurred. Additionally, a committed group of individuals around the United States prayed daily from a prayer calendar mailed out monthly. During one month each year the normal direct-mail fund appeal featured a request for individuals to pray daily for the organization during that month. The volunteers always ended their break time each week by standing, holding hands, and enjoying a time of prayer.

As I list the variety of methods and opportunities used to encourage and support our focus of "No prayer, no results," I'm keenly aware that this list may come across as just that—a list. But each item of that inventory grew out of the desire to put into practice an organizational commitment to prayer. We'll never truly know this side of heaven the full extent of the results brought about by those prayers. Don't overlook what might seem like a simple "Christian" thing to do. Embrace prayer with all your heart. It will start with you.

Begin praying for your volunteers, the ones you have as well as those who are yet to come, your staff, and your organization. Ask for prayer requests. When someone tells you of a need, stop right then and pray for that need. The prayer atmosphere will grow. It's contagious. It will change you and will help create a unique atmosphere when people walk through the door of your organization. It's absolutely true: "No prayer, no results."

To Recap

- Use the opportunity to express appreciation to your volunteers in some special way during National Volunteer Week.
- Have an all-out special event once a year to highlight your thankfulness for your volunteers.
- Find ways to recognize your volunteers on a day-to-day basis.
- Pray! Remember: no prayer, no results.

RESOURCES FOR VOLUNTEERS

Volunteers are the only human beings on the face of the earth who reflect this nation's compassion, unselfish caring, patience, and just plain love for one another.
—Erma Bombeck

I've made suggestions throughout the book to help you launch a successful program benefiting you and your volunteers. This chapter is a combination of all of those examples in full format and several other items you might find useful. The first section is made up of general resources and helpful information. The second section is divided by the chapters in which the material is discussed.

Gifts Source Ideas

The following list identifies great sources for volunteer and staff appreciation gifts:

- Positive Promotions, <www.postivepromotions.com>, 1-800-635-2666. This is a valuable resource. You can sign up to receive a free catalog at this Web site. The catalog includes useful ideas for showing appreciation to volunteers that go beyond gift suggestions.

- <volunteergifts.com>. You'll find merchandise at discount prices designed exclusively for nonprofit organizations such as schools, universities, associations, the military, alumni, hospitals, community development groups, faith-based organizations and other 501C organizations.
- Multi Business Systems, <www.multibusinesssystems.com>, 1-800-776-0061. This is a supplier of printed business forms and promotional products. Printed forms include business cards, mailing envelopes, and computer checks, all deliverable in approximately one week. They personalize bags, pens, mugs, T-shirts, sweatshirts, caps, pencils, key tags, and anything else that says "thanks" to your volunteers or helps those attending your trade show to remember you. Search the Web site for more than 10,000 available items.
- Oriental Trading Company, <www.orientaltrading.com>, has value-priced toys, novelties, party supplies, and crafts.
- Thanks Company, <www.thankscompany.com>. Thanks started approximately ten years ago when the director of a local Abuse Prevention Council couldn't find appropriate thank-you cards for volunteers.

Just to get your creative juices flowing, following is a list of gift ideas that I have used and their general cost, including a wide variety of gifts at reasonable prices. Again, remember to ask about a discount for nonprofit organizations. And, again, every item should include your logo and, if possible, your contact information. Perhaps you can include only your Web site address, but you do need to incorporate some way for people who are interested in your organization to contact you.

You may be able to find a better price on these items; these prices are approximate. As is usually the case, the more you purchase, the lower the price.

- T-shirts—$7 each.

- Polo shirts—$25 each. We gave one to each volunteer the second time he or she came in to serve. Volunteers were easily recognized in their matching shirts.
- Insulated tumblers—$5. These are some of the most popular items we ever gave as gifts. We ordered extras to fill donor requests; they were an enduring favorite.
- Bumper stickers—96 cents. Bumper stickers can say, "I serve at [name of the organization]." Or you can use a quote from the founder or your organization's tagline along with the organization's name.
- Café mugs—starting at $2.75. Beyond using these as gifts for the volunteers and staff, we gave mugs to donors, guests of the organization, and committee members. They were popular, and we purchased several different versions over the years.
- Lapel pins—rectangle-shaped for under $2. The lapel pin is an item that can also be used to recognize that someone is with your organization. I suggest that the lapel pin include just your logo.
- Key chains—full color both sides, for under $2. You can advertise on just one side for less cost. Everyone carries keys, making key chains a useful gift that's a continuous reminder of your organization. A catchy theme expressing your organization's appreciation might be "Our volunteers are the key to our success." That may sound corny, but it works. Themes can also tie in with your appreciation-function decorations.
- Umbrellas—$8. They will be used for years.
- Lunch bags—$4. An insulated bag with a heavy lining about the size of a paper lunch bag.
- Canvas bags—from $4 to $8. We used this gift twice in two different versions because it was so popular. Our human resources department began requesting these to

give to newly oriented stateside and international staff members.

- Compact leatherette organizer with calculator and writing pad—$4. The CEO first saw this item at the volunteer appreciation brunch and thought it was an expensive gift. I told him that except for the polo shirts, I seldom paid over $5 each for appreciation gifts. My goal was to purchase a special gift of the best quality I could find for under $5.

Empowering Leadership Sources

Below is a list of sites that can provide helpful information to encourage and support your volunteer program. These include articles, sample forms, online newsletters, and much more.

- Energize, Inc., <www.energizeinc.com>. Energize, Inc., empowers leaders of volunteers by connecting them to the highest-quality resources available. Management resources include books, professional journals, consulting, online training, and a robust free online library.
- Idealist.org, <www.idealist.org>. This is a volunteer management resource center. Volunteer management professionals do challenging and rewarding work at Idealist, where they're committed to supporting you with resources, tools, and networking opportunities.
- Volunteer Today—The Electronic Gazette for Volunteerism, <www.volunteertoday.com>. The mission of Volunteer Today is to provide free information on the engagement of volunteers through pertinent information on recruiting as well as information and promotion on professional development opportunities for those who work to engage volunteers.
- Service Leader, <www.serviceleader.org>. Service Leader provides information on all aspects of volunteer management, including getting your organization ready to involve volunteers, volunteer screening, volunteer match-

ing, record-keeping and evaluation, legal issues/risk management, volunteer/staff relations, online activism by volunteers, and volunteer management software. A complete online library for nonprofits and for-profits is also available.

- Free Management Library, <www.managementhelp.org/staffing/outsrcng/volnteer/volnteer.htm>. The library provides easy-to-access, clutter-free, comprehensive resources regarding the leadership and management of self, other individuals, groups, and organizations. Over the past ten years it has grown to be one of the world's largest, best-organized collections of these types of resources.

Volunteer Blogs

- Your Volunteers, <www.yourvolunteers.blogspot.com>. This is my blog for those who work with volunteers. Check it out for updated and new ideas, resources, and useful information. Post your ideas too.
- Volunteer, <www.volunteer.wordpress.com>. Mostly used by organizations for postings about their volunteers, their program, or their needs.
- Volunteer Manager, <www.volunteermanager.wordpress.com>. This blog is a site to discuss issues or give and read opinions and even get some advice regarding volunteer management.

Chapter 2

Questionnaire

Last Name _____ First Name _____

Phone number _____ Best time to call _____

Address _____

City, State _____ Zip _____

Birth date: (year not required) _____

Hobbies:

Spiritual Gifts:

Special training/experience:

Work experience:

Days & Time Available: (Check as many as apply)
Days—( ) Monday ( ) Tuesday ( ) Wednesday ( ) Thursday ( ) Friday
Time— _____ _____ _____ _____ _____

Area of interest: (Check as many as apply. If you have any questions about what is involved with any of the areas, please feel free to ask)

Miscellaneous	Office	Software Experience
( ) Group work	( ) Computer work	( ) Word
( ) Working individually	( ) Filing	( ) Excel
( ) Research work	( ) Proofreading	( ) Photoshop (version ___)
( ) Driving to & from airport	( ) Copy work	( ) MS Outlook
___ Modesto	( ) Telephoning	( ) PageMaker (version ___)
___ San Francisco	( ) Fill in on phones	( ) PowerPoint
___ Sacramento	( ) Clerical support	( ) _____
( ) Housing visitors	( ) Bulk mailing work	
( ) Accounting interest	( ) Photo scanning	
( ) Fundraising interest	( ) _____	
( ) Fix-it person		
( ) Set up/take down for events		

( ) Other _____

Comments: (Please use the back of this sheet)

Chapter 3

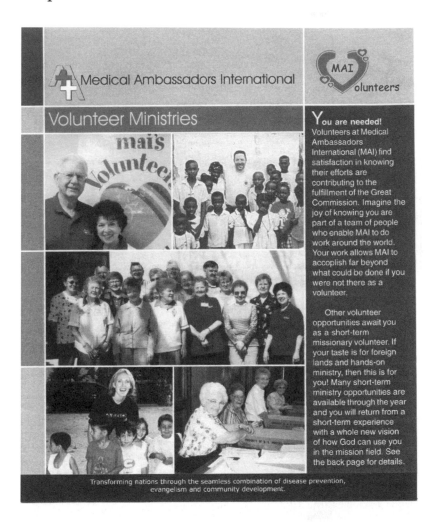

Medical Ambassadors International

MAI Volunteers

Volunteer Ministries

You are needed! Volunteers at Medical Ambassadors International (MAI) find satisfaction in knowing their efforts are contributing to the fulfillment of the Great Commission. Imagine the joy of knowing you are part of a team of people who enable MAI to do work around the world. Your work allows MAI to accoplish far beyond what could be done if you were not there as a volunteer.

Other volunteer opportunities await you as a short-term missionary volunteer. If your taste is for foreign lands and hands-on ministry, then this is for you! Many short-term ministry opportunities are available through the year and you will return from a short-term experience with a whole new vision of how God can use you in the mission field. See the back page for details.

Transforming nations through the seamless combination of disease prevention, evangelism and community development.

Serving close to home

Marshall and Janet Jensen

We had wanted to live our lives "purposely," to do more with our retirement than just travel or play golf. It was our desire to have our lives used for God's work.

We wanted to have a ministry that we could do together. In our retirement years, our desire was to serve as a couple. We met with a Medical Ambassadors International (MAI) representative and were challenged to move from Illinois to Modesto to become part of the "volunteer army" with MAI. It turned out to be the perfect opportunity.

Our greatest joy in our volunteer work at MAI is experiencing the joy of seeing lives touched both spiritually and physically. We are thrilled to know that we are having a part in others coming to the Lord. We really appreciate the ministry that touches people's felt needs as well as the spiritual side.

We wait eagerly to hear about the responses to mailings we work on. We have the privilege of seeing the ministry move ahead because of the response to the mailings. We cherish the times we spend praying for the needs presented in a specific area. We believe that MAI is reaching places and people that no other ministry is reaching, and we are a part of that—we believe we are making a difference.

"...MAI is reaching places and people that no other ministry is reaching, and we are a part of that—we believe we are making a difference."

"I like to volunteer at MAI, knowing that the work is centered on what Christ has called us to do, to fulfill the Great Commission." —Mary

Visit us on the web at www.MedicalAmbassadors.org

109

Opportunities

Volunteer opportunities abound! Use your skills and spiritual gifts in a way that has a direct link to the mission field. By volunteering at the Modesto headquarters you will truly be making a difference.

"I love what the misson stands for and I believe in it whole-heartedly. I love the fellowship with other volunteers ... it is very exciting being a part of MAI and in the service of the King." —Phyllis

Office volunteers:

- Filing
- Copy work
- Telephoning
- Receptionist relief
- Clerical support
- Proofing
- Bulk mailing preparation
- Airport pickup/dropoff
- Washing office windows
- Landscape cleanup

"I look forward to coming to MAI to volunteer. The people have become a great part of my life. It is a real joy to be able to serve the Lord in this way and further the cause of the mission." —Vernita

Transforming nations through the seamless combination of disease prevention, evangelism and community development.

Community Health Evangelism

Our strategy

Community Health Evangelism (CHE) is the key strategy being used by MAI. Three essential qualities make the CHE strategy unique:

The integration of physical and spiritual ministry which changes lives through the leverage of Christ's demonstrated love.

Multiplication through the training of nationals who will transform others, multiplying the results from community to community.

Community ownership of a program which is directed by the villagers themselves with a minimum of resources from the outside. This allows the ministry to continue and expand long after outside assistance has moved to another area.

Learning clean water techniques is a principal component for healthy communities

P.O. Box 576645
Modesto, California
95357-6645
888-403-0600
Fax 209-571-3538

We need YOU!

Consider investing your skills and talents to make a difference for Jesus Christ in the lesser-developed world.

Visit us on the web at
www.MedicalAmbassadors.org

Community Health Evangelism

a strategy of
Medical Ambassadors International

Our purpose

The purpose of Medical Ambassadors International (MAI) is to transform nations through the seamless combination of disease prevention, evangelism, and community development.

Learning through picture books

This is done through mobilizing and training nationals in their own country to minister to their people's physical, spiritual, emotional and social needs. Currently, MAI has over 4,000 paid and volunteer national staff serving in 56 countries.

Opportunities

You can transform nations as an Area Coordinator, representing Medical Ambassadors International (MAI) in an assigned area, guiding, mentoring, and directing the quality of the implementation of MAI's vision, purpose, and Community Health Evangelism (CHE) strategy.

The Area Coordinator's duties are many and varied, from opening new countries and programs for CHE to implementing budgets.

The Area Coordinator must be a mature Christian with a firm conviction of God's leading to Christian service, with generally good physical and emotional health and appropriate education and training. The Area Coordinator must be willing to live overseas in their area of responsibility or annually spend two, three-month periods there.

The Area Coordinator should be able to raise his/her own support.

You can transform nations as a Resource Specialist, utilizing your background in business, agriculture, discipleship, animal husbandry, appropriate technology, and many other areas of transferable skill.

Resource Specialists spend two to four weeks on the field demonstrating to the nationals the techniques that will allow them to become more productive and thus help reduce their dependency on outside help. They make trips to various areas of the world four to six times a year.

The Resource Specialist must be a mature Christian with a firm conviction of God's leading to Christian service, with generally good physical and emotional health and appropriate education and training.

The Resource Specialist should be able to raise his/her own support.

Transforming nations through the seamless combination of disease prevention, evangelism and community development.

Medical Ambassadors International

Volunteer Ministries signup

Close to Home
☐ I am interested in helping at the Modesto home office. Please send me a sign-up sheet so I can tell you about my gifts and interests.

Short-term
☐ I am interested in a short-term ministry opportunity. Please send me information on scheduled trips and how I can get involved.

Important! Please fill in the information on the reverse side.

From

Name _____

Street Address _____

City, State, Zip _____

Telephone ( ) _____

Place stamp here if mailing

Volunteer Coordinator
Medical Ambassadors International
PO Box 576645
Modesto CA 95357-6645

Chapter 4

VOLUNTEER REQUEST FORM

Your Name _____ Today's Date _____

I need volunteer help _____

_____

_____

The best time for them to complete this task would be on _____
(Date)

between _____ and _____ .
       (Time)   (Time)

Deadline _____ .

VOLUNTEER ASSIGNMENT

Volunteer(s) Assigned _____

Volunteer(s) Contacted on _____

They will be here on _____ at _____ .

They will report to _____ .

AFTER TASK IS COMPLETED

Was the task completed to your satisfaction? _____ Comments: _____

_____

_____

_____

Did you remind the volunteer to sign the "Volunteer Book"? Our auditor requires it. _____

Chapter 6

Volunteer Handbook

Organization's Name
Mailing address:
Street address:
Phone:
Fax:
E-mail:
Web site:

Contents

1. Introduction

A. You Are Important!

All volunteers of _____
have significant ministries. Without their faithful service, the work
of _____ personnel would be immea-
surably harder and likely less fruitful.

B. This Is a Christian Office.

Although the day-to-day work schedule includes activities common to most offices, such as typing, accounting, computing, filing, and so on, it's important to remember that these activities
support an international Christian ministry. All personnel are to
follow biblical principles of behavior and conduct.

Volunteers should make a conscious effort to maintain a close and
constant walk with the Lord, to strive for a good working relationship with others, and to practice patience, Christian love, and
forgiveness. By our words and deeds others should see a difference
in our lives.

C. We Have a Purpose!

Our purpose is to glorify God by fulfilling His command to make
disciples of all peoples.

The motto of _____ is _____
_____.

D. Why Guidelines?

Without guidelines, chaos and confusion are commonplace. We all
need guidelines to maintain a well-ordered and organized work
environment. Yet, guidelines that do not serve the needs of all stifle
the work effort. They are neither well-received nor useful.

The following guidelines have been formulated considering each
person's importance, recognizing this is a Christian office, and in
keeping with the organizational purpose that characterizes our
work as ministry.

2. Office Schedule

Office Hours

Regular office hours are from _____ A.M. to _____ P.M., Monday through Friday.

3. General Guidelines

A. Personal Appearance

Cleanliness and a high standard of personal appearance influence the work environment as well as the Christian testimony of the organization.

B. Office Housekeeping

In consideration of others, and of office visitors, everyone is expected to maintain a neat, clean, clutter-free work area. These areas should be as clear as possible at the end of each work day.

C. Telephone Calls and Office Visits

We recognize that you will need to make and receive occasional personal telephone calls during normal office hours. Generally, we discourage incoming calls from family, friends, and associates. Similarly, regular and prolonged office visits by family, friends, and associates should be discouraged.

D. Courtesy and Conversation

Quiet office conversation helps everyone concentrate on his or her own work. Loud talking and laughing hinders the work environment and is distracting when others are occupied in business conversations.

For the sake of courtesy, individuals will wait outside an office or away from a desk when another individual is talking on the telephone. We should also maintain a respectful distance when two or more individuals are talking.

E. Confidentiality

You may occasionally see documents or overhear others discussing sensitive and/or confidential matters. These may pertain to employees, missionaries, missions, churches and/or financial matters or supporters.

It is critical that such information remain confidential.

Should you see or hear something that you believe to be a significant problem or impropriety, you are encouraged as a first step to clarify the issue with the individual involved. Then, if necessary, you may discuss the issue with the _____ and/or the administrator.

F. Concerns and Problems

Even in a Christian organization it is inevitable that occasional interpersonal problems will occur.

If after a brief cooling-off period a more serious conflict lingers, you are encouraged to follow the instructions outlined in Matthew 18:25-27: First, go to your coworker and share your concern. If the two of you cannot resolve the problem, then (and only then) ask the administrator to hear the concerns of both parties in order to mediate a solution.

As Christians, we have an obligation to maintain harmony and good relationships with others. This does not mean we always agree or that suggestions and constructive criticism are not valuable.

What it does mean, however, is we must be able to work together and resolve conflicts with others, bringing honor to the Lord. First Corinthians 13 should be considered.

G. Sexual Harassment

In a Christian office it is our hope that sexual harassment will never occur.

We strive to maintain a working environment free from all forms of sexual harassment or intimidation. Sexual advances (welcomed or unwelcome), requests for sexual favors, the use of obscene or objectionable language, name-calling, or any other action considered offensive, as well as other verbal or physical conduct of a sexual nature, are serious violations of policy and will not be condoned or permitted. Not only is sexual harassment a violation of our policy, but it also violates Title VII of the Civil Rights Act of 1964.

Anyone who is subjected to sexual harassment or intimidation by a fellow volunteer, employee, manager, or supervisor should contact the administrator. All complaints of sexual harassment will be promptly and confidentially investigated.

Any employee, manager, or supervisor who violates this policy will be subject to appropriate disciplinary action up to and including termination.

NOTE: Please use language regarding sexual harassment policies that complies with the laws of your state.

4. Holidays

Scheduled Holidays When the Office Will Be Closed
New Year's Day
Martin Luther King Jr. Day
President's Day
Good Friday (1/2 day, from 12:00 noon)
Memorial Day
Independence Day
Labor Day
Thanksgiving Day
Friday after Thanksgiving
Christmas Eve (1/2 day, from 12:00 noon)
Christmas Day

5. Job Description

A. Job Description for Volunteers
1. Understand the task you undertake.
2. Accept orientation and training appreciatively.
3. Serve faithfully, and report new insights about your work to the volunteer coordinator.
4. Discover the meaning to the total process of which your task is a part.
5. Open yourself to opportunities for growth in skills, self-confidence, love, and responsibility.
6. Contribute to supervision by self-evaluation and a willingness to ask questions.

7. Maintain confidentiality regarding any information gained through your time.
8. Take pride in the volunteer career. It pays handsomely in treasures of the spirit.
9. Know above all things that the staff here loves and appreciates you and your servant heart.

Whatever you do, do all to the glory of God.
—1 Corinthians 10:31

Whatever you do, do it heartily, as to the Lord and not to men, knowing that from the Lord you will receive the reward of the inheritance, for you serve the Lord Christ.
—Colossians 3:23-24

B. Task Descriptions

It is our desire to keep you informed. Below you will find a list of volunteer tasks, a time frame, the number of people needed to complete the task, and a description of what is involved.

1. Cleaning

Dusting in Offices
(As needed, one or two people)
1. Supplies are provided.
2. Dust offices when individuals are gone.
3. Dust one or two areas per visit.
4. Items to be dusted include baseboards, book shelves, desk and countertops, windowsills, as appropriate.

Polishing Woodwork
(This task can be done in conjunction with the dusting.)
1. Supplies are provided.
2. Polish woodwork in the offices of individuals who are gone.
3. Polish in one or two areas per visit
4. Items to be polished include bookshelves, desktops, and countertops.

General Cleaning
(Weekly, one or two people)
1. Supplies will be provided.
2. Floors are to be vacuumed.
3. Trash is to be emptied.

4. Bathrooms are to be cleaned (floors, sinks, toilets).

Washing Windows
(Scheduled basis, one or two people)
1. Supplies will be provided.
2. Wash the inside of all windows and the outside of ground-level windows.

2. Miscellaneous
Missionary Apartment Hostess
(As needed, one person or a couple)
1. Before guest arrives—dust and clean room, provide clean linens (bedding, towels, washcloths, and so on), air out room, prepare welcome basket, check to make sure dishes and utensils and cookware are available and refrigerator is clean.
2. After guest departs—wash linens, clean room thoroughly, and put clean dishes away in appropriate cupboards or drawers. Empty refrigerator of any leftover food or beverages.

3. Office
Bulk mailing work
(As needed, team)
1. Fold material to be inserted into an envelope.
2. Match letters and/or other material to envelopes, and place the letters and/or other material into the envelopes.
3. Send envelopes through bulk mail machine, or hand stamp them (as needed).

Clerical support
(As needed, one person)
Compile information for various trips, information about countries or people, contact lists, reports, maps, and so on.

Computer work
(As needed, one person)
Input information into the computer as needed.

Photocopy work
(Once a week, one person, who could also take care of filing)
At times large amounts of photocopied materials are needed for training booklets, brochures, statistical reports, large

mailings, and so on. Some collating and folding and placing of the material in folders may be needed.

Filing

(Once a week, one person, who could also take care of the photocopy work)

Staff members who have ongoing filing needs should keep their filing in a sorter. The volunteer would complete this task in an office where the filing cabinets are located.

Telephoning

(As needed, one or two people)

1. Fill in as receptionist when someone is ill.
2. Place calls as needed

4. Outside

Lawn care

(Weekly, one person or a couple)

1. Mow.
2. Edge.
3. Blow.
4. Place lawn refuse in trash bin.

Plant flowers

(As needed, one person or a couple)

1. Flowers and/or bulbs provided.
2. Plant flats of flowers and/or bulbs.
3. Weed as needed.

Rake leaves

(Fall, team)

During the fall season, leaves need to be raked on an ongoing daily basis.

Sweep walks

(Fall, team)

This task could be done at the same time as the leaves are raked and perhaps by the same person.

Volunteer Covenant

1. As a volunteer I realize that I am bound by the same ethics as the staff, including confidentiality, honesty, respect, and acceptance of all people.

2. As a volunteer I commit myself to a high standard of performance.

3. As a volunteer I promise to maintain confidentiality regarding any information gained through my volunteer work.

4. As a volunteer I will attempt to be considerate and accepting toward the public, knowing that my attitude is an important part of my involvement with, and reflects upon, the organization.

5. As a volunteer, I will be responsible to the time I have committed.

6. For the benefit of my volunteer work and my own satisfaction and growth, I will bring problems that I encounter to the staff person assigning my work for his or her assistance and direction.

7. As a volunteer, I accept this covenant as my own, looking forward to using my gifts.

_____   _____
Signature   Date

Chapter 7

Nonprofit Organizational Chart Relating to Volunteers Format

CEO
|
Department Director
|
Executive Assistant to Department Director
|
Assistant
|
Lead Volunteer Leadership Couple
|
Assistant/Apprentice Leadership Couple
|
Volunteers

Small Church Organization Chart Relating to Volunteers

Senior Pastor
|
Assistant
|
Volunteer Leadership Team
|
Volunteers

If the church has pastors over different ministries, then the appropriate pastor and his or her assistant, under the senior pastor, should oversee the volunteer leadership team for that ministry.

For Committees

CEO/President
|
Department Director
|
Co-chairs
|
Advisory Committee
|
Staff Liaison
(could be the assistant to the Department Director or CEO)
|
Individual Volunteer

🖐 FREQUENTLY ASKED QUESTIONS AND FREQUENTLY VOICED CONCERNS

Take the attitude of a student: never be too big to ask questions;
never know too much to learn something new.
—Og Mandino

There has been a large amount of information given, but you may still have questions. Following are frequently voiced concerns and frequently asked questions.

Many volunteers don't seem to understand that assuming responsibility comes with volunteering. Many times volunteers at the church where I work fail to show up on a regular basis. How do I express the seriousness of the commitment to potential volunteers in a way that motivates them without scaring them off?

From my own experiences and discussions with others, this is unfortunately a common frustration. It should be addressed by the person at the top—in this case, the senior pastor. Request an appointment with the senior pastor, and come to the meeting with your list of needs. Approach it in a professional way, and be prepared to present your needs—not only in the church office but also the needs in other areas of the church. Pray and think about the meeting well in advance. The goal of the appointment with the senior pastor is to discuss your concerns and possibly encourage him or her to preach a sermon or a series of sermons on spiritual gifts. The purpose of such a message will be to motivate those who are just showing up on Sunday and help them understand that every Christian has a gift that God desires to be used in the Body of Christ.

As an adjunct to the pastor's teaching, spiritual gift tests could be provided with a link from the church's Web site. The tests for both youth and adults can be accessed at <www.spiritualgifts test.com>.[1] For a one-time fee, you can link the test and results information to your Web site. Hard-copy versions of the tests can also be made available for those who do not have computers.

I have tried many times to find a way to handle this frustration without drawing in the senior pastor, but no other way is as effective over the long term as challenging the congregation from the pulpit. When the pastor gets involved, the work of volunteers is accorded a position of respect and importance. There will still be some church members who will continue to sit in the pews and expect everything to be done for them. But there are some who have been unaware of the need because it hasn't been effectively communicated to them.

If the senior pastor doesn't want to become involved, or if you feel you can't go to the senior pastor with your concerns, there is a somewhat useful method you can use, with the pastor's approval, to promote volunteerism in your church. Here are the steps I have taken:

- Put together a bulletin insert and matching posters for classrooms or church bulletin boards that explain and encourage spiritual gifts and their benefit to the church body. This should be short, to the point, including the facts and providing the link on the church's Web site.

- Provide handout copies of spiritual-gift tests for those who are interested in taking the test and don't have computers or prefer not to take the test on the computer.
- The person taking the test should return the test to receive his or her results, giving you the opportunity to make a personal pitch about church needs.
- Link the printout of the individual's spiritual gift(s) to a list of volunteer opportunities within the church. Include contact information for available opportunities, dates, and times volunteers are needed. This could be as simple as a list of your needs with the spiritual or practical gift required listed next to the task.
- E-mail can be a valuable tool. You can send volunteer opportunity information to individuals, particularly those who have the time to serve. The church's weekly or monthly newsletter or electronic newsletter is also a great way to communicate service opportunities and share which spiritual gifts are helpful for various tasks.
- Use the bulletin or bulletin inserts to provide more service opportunities for individuals and list the spiritual gifts suited to the tasks.
- Get permission to make short announcements from the pulpit to explain the need for volunteers and encourage people to take the test and utilize their gifts.
- Schedule an informational and training meeting for all those who think they are interested in using their personal gifts from God. During that meeting you should have additional information available regarding their potential roles and what ways they might use their gifts and talents.

In the event the senior pastor agrees to preach about spiritual gifts from the pulpit, you should be prepared to complement the sermons and provide an action plan for the church body.

Where do I find volunteers?

Before you start the search for volunteers, you must know the qualities you should look for to fill specific needs. In chapter two we looked at the categories of volunteerism and the general characteristics of volunteers in these categories. Use those descriptions to help you pinpoint the kind of people you are seeking.

Chapter three gives pointers on ways to locate those people. The best way to recruit volunteers is by word of mouth or through a personal invitation by someone within your organization or, better still, another volunteer.

How do I talk to them? What should I say?

I know firsthand that most one-assistant offices are so busy with long lists of responsibilities that it's hard to think about what sorts of questions to ask potential volunteers, much less think about training them. So if you're an assistant who feels that, although having a volunteer to help out would be extremely desirable, there's no time to stop and talk to the person, you're probably wondering how the person can be brought up to speed and become helpful to the organization without costing you a ton of time and interrupting your productivity. You're in a get-it-done mode, nose to the grindstone, head down, moving straight ahead.

Balance—that's what you need! A volunteer can help provide that necessary quality in your life. Yes, you'll have to stop and slow down, for a time, to get the volunteer functioning in a way that's helpful to you and the organization. But it will be beneficial for you, even beyond the prospect of getting more tasks done. If you're going one hundred ten miles an hour, I know you don't want to hear this, but you need balance. One way to accomplish this is to slow down, train a volunteer, and allow him or her to help you. How do you talk to a volunteer? You have to stop a minute, look him or her in the eyes, say hello, voice your appreciation, then tell the volunteer what needs to be done.

Where do I put a volunteer in this small space?

I once volunteered for a church office and ended up working with the senior pastor's overhead slides. He used overheads when he preached, and my job was to clean them, create overheads with new illustrations, and file the used ones. The file they belonged in was a cabinet behind the pastor's desk, so I came in on his day off—usually Thursday—and sat at his desk to do my volunteer work. It seemed strange at first, but I was grateful for any unoccupied desk—even for just one morning. Of course, you must ask permission before you use someone else's space.

I've also used lightweight, plastic-topped folding tables in a hallway as a workspace. The small tables are four feet long and great for any open area, and they are especially convenient because they can easily be taken down when not in use and stored beside or behind a file cabinet or in a closet.

For bigger projects, the church foyer is a great place to set up folding tables as a space for volunteers to work on weekday mornings. In one church where I worked, some of the church ladies came in on Friday mornings to put inserts into the bulletins for Sunday. They took over the guest chairs in the reception area. I've also had volunteers work across from me at my desk. They just pulled up a chair and worked away.

The point is that there's always room. But you may have to look at your space with fresh eyes and a creative heart.

I have a detailed list of tasks and people who are interested in volunteering. What's the next step?

You are well on your way. The next step is to see if the people who are interested in volunteering match up with your list of tasks. As an example, let's use the task of grant writing. Grant writing is a specific task that requires explicit knowledge and well-developed skills. I recommend that you request a sample of the person's past work and see if it corresponds with your needs.

Also, ask what the outcome was from the grants the person has written.

The same action would be recommended for the other tasks on your list. Don't take for granted that potential volunteers know how to carry out what they have signed up to do. In addition to interviewing people, ask for samples. If the task requires specialized knowledge or skills, request recommendations.

Are there certain tasks volunteers should be asked to do and some tasks they should not be asked to do? Can you give examples?

Let me ask you a question: What are your needs? As a rule of thumb, I don't ask a volunteer to do anything I myself haven't done or wouldn't be willing to do.

Take the time to evaluate tasks you currently perform that could be delegated to a volunteer; then make a list of them. I kept a plastic inbox in an out-of-sight location and put in it reminders of tasks I couldn't get to immediately, usually things like filing, master calendar updates, address changes, scanning, and so on. That served as my ongoing, ready-made, volunteer to-do list for any volunteer who might show up or for a staff member who was all caught up on his or her own work. When anyone was looking for something to do, I could always accommodate!

Who should train volunteers?

Training can be done by either you or the person who needs the task completed. Once you have a trained and established leadership team, the responsibility of training will be turned over to the leadership. However, for specific, individual tasks you'll still need to have the staff member who requested the volunteer to instruct him or her on the job to be performed.

How do we schedule a volunteer? How far in advance should we ask for a volunteer? How many hours should I expect a volunteer to work?

For large jobs that require numerous volunteers, I think you should give them as much advance notice as humanly possible. For the year-end mailing push at the nonprofit where I worked, we began planning three to four months ahead of the mailing deadline. For volunteer tasks performed by an individual, at least a week's notice is necessary. If you're fortunate enough to have a volunteer assigned to work with you on a long-term basis, work out a schedule together that works best for both of you—once a week, once a month, on a certain day of the week, or whatever you and the volunteer decide. Be sure to consider the time of day the volunteer prefers. It's always a good idea to start the process of getting your volunteers on board as soon as you are aware of the need.

The time for scheduling volunteers should coincide with the scope of the need. It's important to begin by calculating how long you anticipate the task will take to complete. When filling out your request form, let the leadership team know what the job entails and how long it should take so that when they contact the volunteer, they can let him or her know the anticipated length of time it will take to complete the job. In my experience, I've found that a few hours at a time is all you can expect from office workers. I usually set it up so that the largest group of volunteers coming to work on mailings come in at 9 A.M. and finish around noon. When individual volunteers are used, the staff member and volunteer should work out an agreeable timeframe and schedule, but the staff member should always defer to the volunteer and his or her availability.

Our nonprofit organization doesn't really have money in the budget for volunteer gifts. What should I do about that?

The short answer is—find it. It's that important. The long answer is that you may need to give up something else in your budget to have the money for volunteer gifts. Contribute personally, find a donor who's willing to help, locate a vendor that gives nonprofits a discount and ask for the discount. It's important to be selective about the gifts you choose, making sure you get the most quality and quantity for the least amount of money. If your volunteer program will be ongoing, plan ahead by making this expense a part of your annual budget. See the list of volunteer resources in chapter 10.

One of my volunteers has her own way of doing every task, and it's not the right way. She is very vocal about it. I need the help, but I'm almost to the point of dreading the days she comes in. I'm so frustrated! How should I handle this?

Not everyone who volunteers will be a good fit. Don't fret. After spending some time in prayer, if you still feel you've exhausted every means of trying to make the situation work, and the relationship can't be turned around, it may be best to end it. After thinking through how you can word things graciously, sit down with the volunteer and tell her that you feel your arrangement is not working out. Thank her for her time, and maybe even make a few suggestions for possible alternative volunteer service within the organization, if that's possible. Hopefully there will be someone else in your organization who has the need for an enthusiastic volunteer. Choose the staff member carefully, because he or she will need to be able to cope with such a demanding volunteer.

When one coworker was in this situation, her solution was to pray the volunteer out. She didn't want to confront the volunteer, so the staff member's answer was to pray. And it worked!

Another possibility in seeking a solution is to sit down with the volunteer and listen. Perhaps the volunteer has a personal need that requires addressing. She may be in pain because of something completely unrelated to her volunteer tasks and just needs someone to listen. Statistics show that ten to fifteen percent of staff members have severe personal problems. Personal and interpersonal factors account for sixty-five to eighty percent of all terminations.[2] Logic assumes that these percentages would be the same among volunteer workers.

Don't neglect the option of talking with a volunteer leadership team member about your concerns. He or she is there to help the staff in all ways possible, including staff/volunteer interventions. The leadership team member may know the volunteer better than you do and can communicate with him or her without exacerbating the situation.

While help is important, it should not be at the expense of your job and own well-being. As with each of your other volunteers, this person needs to be dealt with lovingly.

We are not a mission organization with staff coming home or visiting from overseas. Who should we enlist to talk to the volunteers and help them get the inside track on what's going on with the organization?

Consider asking your president, marketing director, board member, or even someone your organization has served to speak to your volunteers. If your organization has a mission statement, who put it together? These are some of the people who could talk to your volunteers to help them get a big picture of what the organization does, and they'll be able to illustrate the benefits and objectives of the organization firsthand.

Sometimes the questions are complicated
and the answers are simple.
—Dr. Seuss

STORIES OF SERVICE

I don't know what your destiny will be, but one thing I do know: the only ones among you who will be really happy are those who have sought and found how to serve.
—Albert Schweitzer

As a source of encouragement, here are personal stories of volunteers who share their views, insights, and life-changing volunteering experiences.

Janet and I believe that God created in us the desire to retire, leave Illinois, and serve Him in Modesto, California. This occurred after a speaker from Modesto came to where we were living to do a missions conference. We knew the speaker and his wife from evangelistic services we had attended at our former church.

We went out to lunch with them the Saturday before the conference. Aubrey McGann, the speaker, told us he was working at Medical Ambassadors International (MAI) and encouraged us to think about coming to Modesto to volunteer at MAI. God had prepared our hearts, and we believed God was using him to challenge us to walk by faith. We began praying and seeking God about going.

We had retired, having done what we could to be ready for retirement. We had paid off the mortgage, down-sized our belongings, sold the second car, and gotten our house ready to sell. While we were waiting for the house to sell, we asked God to reveal to us what He would have us do.

Until recently, I don't think I really understood what it was to walk by faith. I'm not an expert even now. I think, though, it means dependence on God and His Spirit to lead and empower me to do what I'm not capable of doing on my own, in my own power.

Janet and I don't want to appeal to you based on our righteousness or because we have so much to offer in service. We believe serving God is a privilege, because He has cleansed and redeemed us by the blood of Jesus Christ.

We struggled with the wait involved in selling our house. We were not getting any younger and had given up serving in our church, not wanting to leave in the middle of a term of service. We felt as if we were in limbo, which is probably not a good evangelical term.

We struggled with feeling alone in our venture of faith, but God had given us our Sunday School class and a few other people to encourage us along the way.

As the time lengthened, we sensed that some people were questioning why our house hadn't sold if God wanted us to go. During this time I read in the Bible about Israel's struggle to possess the land of Canaan. It didn't come easily. God expected the Israelites to go in faith and possess it. I also read that Moses lay prostrate before God for forty days to intercede for Israel (Deuteronomy 9:18-19). There were numerous other scriptural examples. We acknowledged our need of intercession to break through.

Our friends, Scott and his wife, Chris, sensed our discouragement, and friends were asked to come and pray. The following passage is what we prayed for our family and ourselves.

I keep asking that the God of our Lord Jesus Christ, the glorious Father, may give you the Spirit of wisdom and revelation, so that you may know him better. I pray also that the eyes of your heart may be enlightened in order that you may know the hope to which he has called you, the riches of his glorious inheritance in the saints, and his incomparably great power for us who believe (Ephesians 1:17-19, NIV).

Our Prayer: *Dear Heavenly Father, we love you and seek your help. We want your will in our lives and your hand on our future. Please lead and empower us to walk in faith. We believe you have led us to go to Modesto, California. Please sell our house and lot. Go before us to prepare the right house in the right price range in Modesto. Fulfill every good purpose of ours and every act prompted by our faith in Christ. May we glorify you in our lives. Become great in us. Give us an enlarged ministry. Fill and empower us by your Holy Spirit, and may our faith express itself in love!*

It took a year-and-a-half to sell the house. An interesting thing occurred during that time: The second realtor divided our house and lot. We felt sure the person who bought our house would offer to buy our lot dirt cheap. God intervened and sold the lot separately, and we ended up with the price we wanted for both the house and lot in the first place.

We served at MAI for a total of four years: two-and-a-half years as volunteer coordinator assistants and the last year-and-a-half as volunteer coordinators. One of the blessings we enjoyed was the friendship of a faithful volunteer couple, Ken and Jan. We meshed well; his mechanical skills with machinery complemented my organizational skills.

—Marshall and Janet Jensen

* * *

I've been a volunteer for a long time. However, my volunteering began in earnest when I heard a plea for someone knowledgeable about construction to go to Italy through a church denomination to help with some construction work there. There was a camp that was once a mill where grain was ground for farmers. The denomination took it over and created a camp for churches in the area to use for meetings, picnics, and other functions.

Before arriving at the camp, four of us attended an orientation introducing us to missionary work. Then we flew to Rome and traveled to the camp, located in a town outside Naples. Our job was to build a second story on a 900-year-old building. We completed the task and added a roof before we returned home. I went back several more times to serve for two- to four-week intervals. I even took my daughter along on one of my visits. It was a real blessing to help where I could.

In 1997 the city of Modesto, California, flooded after unseasonably warm weather melted the snow pack in the mountains and sent torrents of water into the reservoirs and lakes. Water was released from the dams to prevent them from breaking. The Stanislaus River overflowed its banks, pouring water into the lower area. A call went out for volunteers to help clean up the devastating flood. About 600 volunteers showed up. After we each identified our skills, I was asked to drive a forklift. I had worked in an almond processing plant using a forklift. After each job I would find another group still working and join them until it was time to go home. This work went on for the rest of the summer. I think I worked on ten or twelve homes doing roofing, Sheetrock, and many other tasks.

Toward the end of the summer the director of the local gospel fellowship asked me if I would like to become a missionary and go out doing the kinds of things I had been doing all summer, helping other missionaries. That was a great idea, and I applied as a missionary with them.

On December 4 I received a call from a missionary in Rosarito, Mexico, asking me to help with some construction on a house for the pastor and his wife that needed to be finished. I was off to a new adventure.

Since that time, I've been to Mexico many times, helping other missionaries with projects. Once when I was coming down a hill, the motor mounts on my truck broke, and I coasted down the hill. I went into an auto parts store and, not speaking Spanish, did my best to let them know I needed to use the phone. About that time a man came into the store—he recognized me and shouted out, "Wally!" I had worked with him the previous year. He got a missionary friend to come tow my truck to be fixed. Later I was able to help him add a room to his little two-room house.

I volunteered to work at the Bible Institute outside Mexicali, Mexico, doing everything from repairing a stove to fixing chairs to installing doors and windows to painting.

From Mexico I went to Montana, where I helped at a Christian ranch, then on to help missionaries build a log cabin and to roof the church where they served.

I also went to Florida to help rebuild homes destroyed by hurricanes.

Everywhere I've gone I've found things I could do to help my friends. On a trip with my daughter to a convention, we stopped at a friend's home, and I installed a ceiling fan for her. I get so much pleasure from helping others. Many times they don't have the funds to hire someone to help them. Other times it's just something that needs to be done, and I'm available.

Since I've been "retired," I've been so blessed when I help others. I would advise anyone who has the talent or skill to do a certain task to use it to help others. He or she will receive a great blessing just from the satisfaction of helping someone else.

I praise God for letting me do this kind of work for the last ten years. As long as He gives me strength and good health, I'll continue to volunteer my services.

—*Wally Sanford*

✽ ✽ ✽

My daughter was working in Washington, D.C., and on one of my visits to her we made plans to spend some of our time volunteering together. We were made aware of a need with the United Service Organizations (USO) and decided to help them provide drinks and snacks for Marines during a marathon.

The morning of the marathon was cold and rainy, and the hot coffee and hot chocolate we served were a welcome treat for the men and women in the armed forces. We were thankful that the rain stopped for most of the time we were there. However, toward the end of the race the wind and rain came back. A few of the Marines got a tent and put it over the food table. In order to keep it in place, they stayed on duty, one at each pole of the tent, standing and holding the tent up until the last Marine had a chance to receive a drink or snack, and our job was done. What a sight, what a day, what a rewarding service! And we in turn were grateful for their service to us.

—Esther Bradfield

✳ ✳ ✳

I love to volunteer. There's a sense of freedom in giving one's gifts and talents to an organization to help it accomplish its purposes.

I was asked to host the opening of a television program with my pastor. His wife had been hosting with him, but she didn't enjoy being in the limelight. I agreed to help because I love my pastor and his wife, and also because I thought I would enjoy hosting with him before a television audience—and I did.

Before long I was asked to tape a series of four weekly programs called "Focus on Women." The program was a hit and ran for several years. The show was composed of three women, and we discussed various issues that challenge women in the world today.

The television audience was invited to call in and suggest topics they wanted us to discuss. We sometimes invited guests to come on the show, and at other times the three of us would discuss an issue, always from the biblical point of view.

I suppose it was because I enjoyed it so much that they began to ask me to host other programs. Some weeks I hosted three or four programs. While each was only an hour in length, it took two or three hours to tape it, due in part to various technical challenges.

I've also volunteered to teach various classes. Sometimes I've filled in for another teacher who had to miss, and sometimes I've taught a series that lasted several months. But I always try to volunteer whenever something comes into my sphere that I'm able to do. It's one way of giving back to the Lord for all He does for me every day. It's also a wonderful way to give back for all that I've been given from others. I think the phrase for it is "paying it forward."

It's very freeing, because I know in my heart that I'm doing something for someone else with no remuneration—just giving a part of me to others. There's a very real sense of fulfillment in giving to others to fill a need they can't provide for themselves.

I've been given so much from other women. God has brought just the right woman into my life to complete any task I couldn't do myself. I can only surmise that because I've tried to be so generous in giving my time that He is in turn being very generous by sending others to me.

I've learned that to give freely is the only way to live a truly rewarding life!

—*Peggy Britt*

* * *

From November 2005 through December 2006 I had the pleasure of serving as volunteer coordinator for a small non-profit organization in Boise, Idaho. Faith in Action of Boise was originally begun with the assistance of a modest three-year start-up grant from a foundation, sponsor of a ten-year initiative to provide seed money to qualified organizations wishing to assist the nation's elderly. The focus of these grants was to help seniors throughout the nation maintain their independence and remain in their homes as long as possible. In addition to the initial funding, the foundation provided promotional materials and a recruiting/ training video.

Faith in Action of Boise is privileged to have one of the most dedicated, energetic, and committed boards I've ever encountered. Drawn from individuals representing various senior-focused local businesses and faith communities, these individuals have worked tirelessly and with immense enthusiasm to raise funds for the director's salary and general office expenses, as well as providing a variety of services and support in numerous aspects of the operation.

From its inception, two large mainline churches located in downtown Boise have come alongside Faith in Action to support the work of helping area seniors in various ways. A Presbyterian church in Boise has been generous in providing limited financial support, a conference room for monthly board meetings, and an annual luncheon and special program for all the organization's volunteers. In addition, a sizeable number of church members have stepped up to volunteer either on a routine basis or an as-needed basis. This church also sponsors an Alzheimer's Caregivers Support Group that meets one Saturday morning each month and is open to the community.

A local Methodist church has also worked in a complementary way by sponsoring and providing facilities for a weekday Alzheimer's day-care program that gives family caregivers some needed respite. Several church members, both male and female, are also long-term active volunteers with Faith in Action.

Other area faith communities and businesses have been sources of volunteer help or other assistance. For instance, a local plumbing contractor provides occasional help for low-income seniors with plumbing problems. The owner of a local pharmacy has been a resource for information about developments in research and information about medications for individuals with Alzheimer's disease or other memory-loss conditions.

In addition, a local Lutheran church, a presence in downtown Boise for more than one hundred years, provides office space and other forms of support, including several wonderful volunteers, for Faith in Action.

From its inception, Faith in Action of Boise has recruited volunteers primarily from area faith communities of many denominations. This is accomplished by making short presentations about the work of the organization and the need for volunteer assistance during the morning service or at other services or meetings at various area churches. Church members are given an informational brochure as they enter the service that explains the origin, the mission, and the needs of the organization. Following these short appeals, the presenters make themselves available in the church lobby to answer questions about the organization and its needs.

All new volunteers are required to attend an introductory training session before beginning their service assisting senior members of the community. Each person selects the frequency and type of services he or she prefers to provide from a list that includes occasional assistance with household cleaning, small household repairs, yard work, providing a few hours of respite for housebound caregivers, walking with able seniors, assistance with grocery shopping, and providing transportation to medical appointments, among other requests. Faith in Action also maintains a list of individuals who are willing to provide occasional assistance on an as-needed and availability basis. Unfortunately, there are always far more requests for help than personnel are able to provide, which can be very frustrating and disheartening. A recent source of temporary volunteer help for Faith in Action has been students from Boise State University. These students come from various classes that require a specific number of hours of volunteer service from each student. During the first week of the semester, the students are provided with a list and short description of the work of various local agencies and required to select one. This assignment constitutes a substantial percentage of their final grade. As one of several local options, we were always extremely pleased to be selected as the service organization of choice by many students, and our young volunteers were especially popular with our elderly care recipients.

Fundraising has been planned, organized, and manned primarily by board members, assorted family members, and volunteers. For several years the major fundraising event was a weekend white elephant sale of donated items, ranging from jewelry, books, furniture, appliances, clothing, household items, and other items. Although the sale was very successful, the event took an immense amount of effort, energy, and preparation. In the past few years other fundraising activities have been tried with varying degrees of success, but Faith in Action is often in competition for funding and workers with numerous other worthy organizations. Nevertheless, my experience with this small organization was one of the most enjoyable experiences of my life.

—Wanda Matthews

✳ ✳ ✳

On the tenth anniversary of the date I received Christ, I volunteered my summer to serve on a short-term mission trip with Greater Europe Mission. My assignment was in Belgium. I didn't know one person among the one hundred twenty team members distributed throughout Europe.

Once the Belgian team of sixteen members arrived in the country, we spent the first three days in what was fun, but we later learned it was a filtering process. We were divided into three groups, then sent into town on a scavenger hunt that consisted of finding a specific bus stop, a store where we were to purchase a list of common items, asking for the time, and finding the train station and the cost and track required for a trip to Brussels at a designated time.

On the third day we were separated into different groups, and the area for the scavenger hunt was expanded to other towns. One place we had to locate was a certain military cemetery for American soldiers and a particular soldier's gravestone. Then we had to note the age of the soldier. It was a very moving experience walking silently up and down the rows of white gravestones reading the names. We realized that most of these men were younger when they were killed than we were at the time we searched the cemetery. It was sobering.

After three full days of these new experiences, the team met again with our missionary leader. At this meeting we learned our little scavenger hunts were really a test of skills and leadership ability. It didn't feel like a test. To my surprise, I was named leader of a group of thirteen team members.

Our base was an old, castle-like, seven-story building that housed the Greater Europe Mission's Bible Institute in Belgium. Two student work teams did all the jobs required to keep the institute running in tip-top shape. Belgium is made up of two distinct halves: the northern half is Dutch, and the southern half is French-influenced. The same was true of the work teams that keep the institute running: one team was Dutch, and a separate team was French. During the summer months, these two teams ran week-long family camps. One week would be a Dutch family camp, and another week would be a French family camp. These family camps brought together many Christians from all over Belgium, the Netherlands, Germany, and France who did not have other believers to fellowship with in their hometowns.

To relieve the Dutch and French work teams to be able to run the family camps, the short-term missionary team members came in during the summer and took on their jobs. The task placed before me required me to spend time with each team and learn their jobs so I could teach each new work team member. This included the Americans and volunteers from other nations who had come to work at the institute from countries such as Vietnam and throughout Africa. I also had to arrange work schedules, assign jobs, teach the tasks, lead the daily morning devotions, and review the day's responsibilities.

The jobs included washing all the dishes for three meals every day for between one hundred fifty to three hundred people or more. We cleaned all the public areas, which included mopping and sweeping the floors. One big job was sweeping the large marble stairway on our knees with a whisk broom and dust pan. It was during one of these cleaning sessions that a non-Christian family member attending the family camp asked, "Who are these people who are willing to clean the steps I'm walking on?" The camp counselor said, "They're Americans who paid their way to be here." The person couldn't believe people would be willing to do that. Out of this experience, the camp counselor was able to share Christ with the individual, and she asked Christ to be her Lord and Savior.

What an incredible summer that was, full of many unexpected opportunities, challenges, and rewards! The leadership position was a complete surprise to me. I believe your gifts will identify themselves. They will ooze out. I wasn't trying to hold my gifts back. I wasn't really thinking about it. I wanted to just be me and was open to being used in whatever way God wanted to use me.

—Denise

✋ SERVANTHOOD

In this chapter I will share with you a lesson plan on the subject of servanthood that's designed for you to share early-on with your volunteer leadership team. If you already have an established leadership team, you can use it to further strengthen what's already in place or set your volunteer leadership on a new path.

Servanthood is an important topic to discuss at team meetings. I suggest you touch on it briefly in every meeting and review it more thoroughly at least once a year.

❊ ❊ ❊

Opening comment. Rick Warren has made the following statement regarding servanthood: "There will always be more people willing to do great things for God than there are people willing to do the little things. The race to be a leader is crowded, but the field is wide open for those willing to be servants."[1]

What is your reaction to that statement? Reading Warren's statement aloud and then asking for reactions to it should lead to a bit of preliminary discussion and food for thought. You may want to discuss it in depth later. The goal is to get people talking about the topic of servanthood.

Why do you volunteer? This question should be an easy one for team members to answer and will provide you with insight into why they have chosen to work with your organization. Let everyone talk and share his or her personal motivation for volunteering.

"People shouldn't volunteer to please themselves or the organization. They should be excited about working for the Lord! This mind-set usually takes care of attitude problems" (Lowell, long-time volunteer and volunteer leadership team member).

After reading Lowell's statement, do you agree with it? Why or why not? Reflecting upon this statement will take your discussion closer to the point of the lesson. Lowell has hit the mark with the focus of his volunteerism. You want to get your leadership team members to think about who or what they're volunteering for. The motivation behind each act of volunteerism is important.

1. Jesus, Our Example

For even the Son of Man did not come to be served, but to serve, and to give His life as a ransom for many.
—Mark 10:45 NIV

Service, by definition, is an action to benefit another. It involves people working together to make an impact for good in their neighborhoods, communities, or the world. Mark 10:45 provides a clear understanding of the meaning of the term *servant*. The words *servant, service,* and *serve* occur well over 1,100 times in the Bible. Individuals are described as servants of others or servants of God.

In the New Testament the word *servant* is frequently used to designate a master's slave (one bound to him), but also to describe a follower of Christ (a bond slave of Christ). The term expresses a relationship of absolute dependence in which the master and the servant stand on opposite sides, the former having an absolute claim, the latter having total commitment.

How do you define the term *serve?* Mark 10:45 provides the group with a good understanding of *servant.* See if the group can put the verse into their own words.

How did Jesus serve? Mark 10:45 answers this question too. But you want your team members to answer in their own words. Encourage them to talk by asking them to explain their answers.

 _____

Volunteer Activities for Men vs. Women

The largest percentage of male volunteers serve as coaches or referees, with the second category falling to transportation, and then fund-raising. For women the largest percentage falls in the category of tutoring/teaching, followed by fund-raising and then distributing or serving food. One interesting fact is that the lowest category for men to volunteer is distributing or serving food and the lowest percentage for women is in the area of coaching.

—*United States Department of Labor Bureau of Labor Statistics*

2. We Are His Servants

Ask the team members to turn to John 12:26. Then ask one person to read it aloud: "If anyone serves Me, let him follow Me; and where I am, there My servant will be also. If anyone serves Me, him My Father will honor."

Ask another member to read aloud Colossians 3:24: "Knowing that from the Lord you will receive the reward of the inheritance; for you serve the Lord Christ."

How will other volunteers and staff (the world) know we are His servants? Lowell's earlier statement deserves repeating here: "People shouldn't volunteer for themselves or the organization. They should be excited about working for the Lord! This mind-set usually takes care of attitude problems."

Our service is for Him, not for any individual. It's not for the organization or even for the future reward God has promised. We serve for our Lord Jesus Christ.

Ask your team members for examples of servanthood they have seen demonstrated by other volunteers or even members of the leadership team. This is not a time for them to share examples about themselves. If they start talking about their own service, point them again to Mark 10:45 and the example of Christ. It's not about them—it's about Christ and others.

3. Characteristics of a Servant

Love

Read Galatians 5:13 as a group: "You, brethren, have been called to liberty; only do not use liberty as an opportunity for the flesh, but through love serve one another."

How do we demonstrate love as volunteers? Ask participants to give examples they have witnessed or how they think love might play out among the volunteers and between volunteers and staff.

Do you know of examples in which love has not been shown? Bring those up, and ask how the situation could have been changed if handled with love.

Faithfulness

Ask someone to read Matthew 25:21: "His lord said to him, 'Well done, good and faithful servant; you were faithful over a few things, I will make you ruler over many things. Enter into the joy of your lord.'"

What are the "few things" God has put in your life in which you could demonstrate faithfulness? What does faithfulness have to do with being a volunteer? How can faithfulness be valuable to an organization? This discussion gives you the opportunity to talk about being on time, following through with assignments, finishing an assigned task completely, and more.

Not Quarrelsome, Gentle, Able to Teach, Patient

Ask the group to turn to 2 Timothy 2:24. Then ask a volunteer to read the verse: "A servant of the Lord must not quarrel but be gentle to all, able to teach, patient."

How should you handle disputes or problems between volunteers, staff, or in completing a task? Ask leadership about the problems that have occurred and the ways in which they have attempted to resolve them. What has worked, and what needs improving?

Following are useful principles to use as reminders for the team:

- Before addressing a problem with an individual volunteer, ask him or her to come with you so you can talk in privacy away from the working volunteer group.
- Listen to what the volunteer has to say, and ask questions as needed for clarity.
- Make every effort to reinforce the servanthood concept and how that concept can be applied in each situation.

Where Are People Volunteering?

The largest percentages of volunteer activities are performed within religious organizations. This is true for both men and women. The second largest group is educational facilities.

—*United States Department of Labor Bureau of Labor Statistics*

Conclusion: Your Attitude Is the Key

Chuck Swindoll made the following statement in his book *Strengthen Your Grip*:

The longer I live the more I realize the impact of attitude on life. Attitude, to me, is more important than facts. It is more important than the past, than education, than money, than circumstances, than failures, than successes, than what other people think or say or do. It is more important than appearance, giftedness or skill. It will make or break a company . . . a church . . . a home.

The remarkable thing we have is a choice every day regarding the attitude we will embrace for that day. We cannot change our past. We cannot change the fact that people will act in a certain way. We cannot change the inevitable. The only thing we can do is play on the one string we have, and that is our attitude.[2]

Talk to the group about how a person's attitude can make all the difference. If you have a personal example about the benefits of a good attitude, it would be powerful to share it with the group. Do the team members have any examples? Ask them to talk about them.

Memory Verse

"For even the Son of Man did not come to be served, but to serve, and to give His life as a ransom for many" (Mark 10:45 NIV).

Ask everyone to read the verse aloud together. This is the key verse to an attitude of servanthood. It illustrates the purpose and the goal for your leadership team, volunteers, and staff.

Additional Resources for Servanthood Study

- Improving Your Serve: The Art of Unselfish Living, by Charles R. Swindoll
- Conformed to His Image/The Servant As His Lord, 2 Volumes in 1, by Oswald Chambers
- The Practice of the Presence of God, by Brother Lawrence

Handout
Servanthood Study

Opening Comments
Why do you volunteer?

1. Jesus, Our Example
Key verse: Mark 10:45
How do you define the term serve?

How did Jesus serve?

2. We Are His Servants
- John 12:26
- Colossians 3:24

How will other volunteers and staff (the world) know we are His servants?

3. Characteristics of a Servant
- **Love**: Galatians 5:13

- **Faithfulness:** Matthew 25:21

- **Not quarrelsome, gentle, able to teach, patient:** 2 Timothy 2:24

Conclusion: Your Attitude Is the Key

Memory Verse: Mark 10:45, NIV

For even the Son of Man did not come to be served, but to serve, and to give His life as a ransom for many.

NOTES

Chapter 1

1. *MetroWest Daily News*, Framingham, Mass.
2. The Barna Group, "Church Attendance", <www.barna.org>.
3. Major Religions Practiced in the United States chart, 2004 Yearbook of American and Canadian Churches; American Religious Identity Survey (ARIS) 2001, <http://encarta.msn.com/media_701500471/major_religions_practiced_in_the_united_states.html>.
4. National Center for Charitable Statistics, Number of Nonprofit Organizations in the United States, 1996-2006, <http://nccsdataweb.urban.org/PubApps/profile1.php?state=US>.

Chapter 2

1. Reprinted with special permission of Independent Sector, a nonprofit, nonpartisan coalition of charities, foundations, and corporate philanthropy programs whose mission is to advance the common good by leading, strengthening, and mobilizing the independent sector, <http://www.independentsector.org/programs/research/volunteer_time.html>.

Chapter 3

1. <http://www.nationalservice.gov/about/role_impact/history.asp>.

Chapter 5

1. <http://www.nationalservice.gov/about/role_impact/history.asp>.

Chapter 6

1. <http://www.nationalservice.gov/about/role_impact/history.asp>.

Chapter 7

1. <http://www.nationalservice.gov/about/role_impact/history.asp>.

Chapter 11

1. <http://www.spiritualgiftstest.com/>. The Spiritual Gifts Test includes free tests for youth and adults on their web site.
2. Health Partners, EAP-Employee Assistance Programs, <http://www.healthpartners.com/portal/e1626.html>.

Chapter 13

1. Rick Warren's Ministry Toolbox e-newsletter 367, 12/10/2008
2. Reprinted by permission, Charles R. Swindoll, *Strengthening Your Grip* (Nashville: Thomas Nelson, 2003). All rights reserved.

expand discipleship and build relationships through a successful small group program

Successful Small Groups is filled with everything you need to launch and manage a small group program. By examining the best practices of several successful small group programs, author Teena Stewart reveals ways to promote and multiply groups, write group guidelines, train leaders, motivate groups to minister to others, and much more. Whether you're planning to begin a program or wanting to improve an existing one, this valuable resource gives you the skills and information you need to approach small group leadership development like a seasoned pro.

Successful Small Groups
By Teena M. Stewart
ISBN: 978-0-8341-2337-3

BEACON HILL PRESS
OF KANSAS CITY

Organize and Enhance the Operational Side of Your Church's Ministry

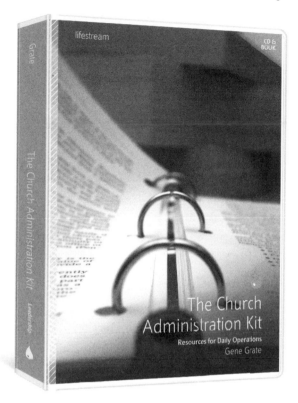

This effective organizational tool helps churches handle the operational side of church ministry. Convenient and practical, it offers guidelines, training helps, templates, suggestions, and practices to enhance efficiency and successfully manage administrative duties and tasks.

With *The Church Administration Kit* and its included CD, you'll receive:
- General job descriptions and office guidelines
- Performance evaluations for pastoral staff and ministry assistants
- Project development and management planning forms
- Policies and procedures for a variety of ministries

The Church Administration Kit
By Gene Grate
ISBN: 978-0-8341-2386-1

BEACON HILL PRESS
OF KANSAS CITY